Morris Minor

MORRIS MINOR

THE BIOGRAPHY

SIXTY YEARS OF BRITAIN'S FAVOURITE CAR

MARTIN WAINWRIGHT

To Penny,
for saying 'Yes' across the gearstick
of UMU 431 F in 1978
and for everything since

REFUSE DISPOSAL(AMENITY)ACT 1978
(ROAD TRAFFIC REGULATION ACT 1967)

Ealing
London Borough

24, Uxbridge road,
London W5 2BP.
Tel: 01-579 2424 ext 3471

TO THE OWNER OF THIS VEHICLE

REGISTRATION NO: *U M U   4 3 1 F*

N O T I C E is hereby given that in the opinion of the aboved named Authority this vehicle is in such a condition that it ought to be destroed and if it is not removed on the expiration of 7 days from the date of this Notice the Council will take it away for destruction.

Dated this *28* TH day of *APRIL* 19 *83*

CHIEF OFFICER WORKS

Contents

Introduction

TO HAVE ONE IS TO LOVE ONE. That sounds soppy, I know, especially when we are talking about a mass-produced car, but it has been so for at least four generations now. I have particular reasons to believe it, as the single most important decision of my life was taken in a Morris Minor, but this book stacks up the wider evidence, from Pease Pottage to Ulan Bator, that the claim is true.

Not just that, either. The Minor has firmly established itself as the most iconic of all British cars, ever. As recently as February 2008 it beat the Mini, the Rolls Royce and the Triumph Spitfire to the top of yet another poll, conducted for the website motorinsurance.co.uk by National Opinion Polls. The cultural world has embraced the little, rounded runabout as eagerly as the social world. Noddy drives a Minor lookalike, and James Bond travels in a Traveller in *Thunderball*. A 'sense' of the Morris Minor is everywhere, and no one needs to be prompted by reminders of what the car actually looks like: it has entered our unconscious because of its long and varied role in sixty years of real life.

The first generation to fall for the Minor was my parents', young in the late 1940s and eager to rebuild a world which had been harrowed by the Second World War.

Everything in them looked for the kindness, warmth and gentle concern for others that the dictatorships had so nearly destroyed. When Lord Nuffield issued primary-coloured advertisements for the new little car from Morris Motors, solid but soft-looking, cheap but made to last, then ordinary, decent family people reached for their wallets.

The second generation is my own, students in the 1960s and 1970s on grants so generous that we could use them to buy cool clothes, Top Twenty vinyl and even a deposit on a second-hand, good-condition Minor costing less than £60. There were masses on the market, all of them supposedly from careful owners. There has seldom been a friendlier car for a learner, or one less-resented by other drivers, even when a long-haired teenager was at the Moggy's wheel. They were blessedly easy to start – the crank handle was a piece of simple genius – or to repair, with a stocking for the fanbelt, or a screwdriver and wire wool for a temporary decoke.

The third generation is busy these days behind those abnormally large steering wheels. These are the enthusiasts who buy and restore old Minors and take them on enormous excursions – thirty or more in a convoy – to rallies here and overseas. Check out the internet for the staggering number and enthusiasm of Morris Minor Owners' clubs and the intensity of their knowledge of the cars. Split-screen, side- and overhead-valve engines, semaphore indicators or blinkers: it is all meat and drink to them, or grease and oil.

And the fourth generation? It is thriving thousands of miles away, in the Indian sub-continent, where the Minor is an unremarkable feature of daily life, a workhorse, taxi or family car that can be mended by a jobbing mechanic almost anywhere it chooses to break down. Sri Lanka, in particular, is a stronghold, and on the outskirts of Galle in the south of the island two small factories make body panels for British renovation enthusiasts, who can order pretty much everything else from suppliers at home. In so doing, the little plants keep alive hopes that fifth and future generations may in due course enjoy Minor motoring.

There are three other reasons to believe this will happen. First, the abiding strength of the principles behind the car's design. The Minor's main creator, Sir Alec Issigonis, is often credited with coining the description of a camel as a horse designed by committee. There are other claimants of that honour, but I hope it was Issigonis, because the saying is so appropriate for the Morris Minor. Sir Alec's genius was tempered by the common sense of practical colleagues such as Vic Oak and Reg Job, as well as the post-war economic squeeze and the famous 'poached egg' reservations of Lord Nuffield. As a result, the car ended up as a compromise, not entirely gainly but brilliantly adaptable to circumstances, and, like a camel, it has always plodded tirelessly on.

Secondly, the affection; here I can step aside to allow a practical chap from Unipart, Patrick Fitz-Gibbon, to tell you that the sentimental claims are true. Cajoling the Church of England's high command when they were dubious about allowing the Archbishop of Canterbury's Morris Minor to enter the 1980 rally in the Himalayas, he put the prospects of national interest and support like this:

'There is not one person in the country who has not ridden in a Morris Minor at some time in their life or known someone who has owned one. It is universally loved as a friendly sort of car.'

Finally, the chances of a New Minor. Instead of the diminished UK car industry, the power to decide on reviving the marque has moved since the takeover of MG Rover by the state-owned Nanjing Car Company to the Chinese ministries of industry and transport in Beijing. Is it curious or alarming that the fate of an English icon rests so far away and with the Chinese government? Far from it. Remember who gave the world tea.

More on that in due course; but meanwhile, I would like to thank everyone who gave me their time, hospitality, memories and/or a look inside, underneath or into the boot and bonnet of their Morris Minors. Rather than list them here, let's meet them as we travel along. Special thanks also to Graham Coster of Aurum Press, whose idea this was, and to his colleague Dan Steward, who supervised production. Also to John Wheelwright, for spotting infelicities and bungles in the manuscript, and to Penny, my wife and Minor mate, who used her exceptional skills as a former chief sub-editor of *Cosmopolitan* on the proofs. Marie Lorimer not only indexed the book but gave me a happy ending (see page 227). I have benefited greatly from reading the books and websites described in the select bibliography and from browsing some of the millions of other references to the Minor online. That is the way to go, if this book whets your appetite for more.

Chapter 1
A Marriage of Minors

I claim my saloon Morris Minor
For petting just couldn't be finer.
But for anything hotter
A Traveller has gotta
Be found. It's a total recliner.

Traditional

 MY FIRST CAR WAS A MORRIS MINOR. I had managed to sponge off my parents for a while after passing my driving test, borrowing their Triumph Herald from time to time, but that was inevitably a temporary arrangement, practicable only while I was living at home in Leeds. I enjoyed it, especially the minimal space between first and reverse on the floppy gearstick, which made journeys exciting. In a boy-racer moment I beat someone off the lights at the bottom of Infirmary Street in what is now Millennium Square. Except that I had slipped into reverse and so shot off backwards, luckily into empty space. The other car's driver was so surprised that he stopped to find out where I had gone.

A motorbike was briefly the answer, but that had the

twin disadvantages of being cold and anti-social. None of us took the bike-riding test, which was scorned in those student revolution days as an Establishment way of getting money, because you had to pay each time, and no one knew anyone who had passed on their first attempt. On L-plates you were not allowed to carry passengers, and the police were vigilant wherever there were students. I was caught, and, while my friend was done for riding pillion on an L-plate bike, I was convicted of aiding and abetting, counselling, soliciting and procuring: a badge of shame which I wore with wrongful pride.

So it had to be four wheels, and for less than £100 – and that meant waiting until I got a job. The day came, and as a young journalist on the *Bath & West Evening Chronicle*, I started looking at the small ads in my own paper. I havered over an Austin A35, which was on offer in Combe Down at a very reasonable price and had sentimental attractions for me. My great aunty Kate had one, called Honey, which she drove round Leeds in a carefree fashion on her work for the Girl Guides and Methodist Sunday school at Roscoe chapel. She was caught on several occasions turning the wrong way or missing a traffic light (in days of much quieter roads) and was, as they say, known to the magistrates. But her evident good works and a very sweet nature (and face; she was a spinster only because the love of her life died in the 'flu after the First World War) meant that she avoided serious punishment. Honey also played a part in softening the magistrates. She (for, like a ship, she seemed to be of that gender) was named after her colour; and, like a Morris

Minor, she was curvaceous with big headlamps resembling eyes.

But then a Minor appeared in the *Chron*'s small ads, and I went to see it, on one of Bath's many steep hills winding up to the Georgian terrace named, with every justification, Perfect View. Like all my generation, I was fond of Morris Minors although I had not been in many. An uncle and aunt had a series of Travellers, but they were always too full of their six children, potties and all, to tempt me in. The only trip which had stuck in my mind was in a very different Traveller – in Rhodesia, where in 1967 I taught between school and university and went on marathon weekend hitch-hikes. Almost all of these led to lifts with partisans or opponents of Ian Smith, who had declared independence illegally two years earlier. An English teenager was just the audience they wanted to explain why their views were right. The Traveller was a glorious exception. It belonged to a Chinese couple who picked me up between Bulawayo and Que Que and passed the long journey in friendly silence. They just turned occasionally from their front seats to smile at their dusty guest in the back. It was a wonderful Minor. There were thick, tasselled curtains on the side and rear windows, a red lantern with gold tassels swaying from the rooflight, and a small Buddha behind smoking joss sticks in the ash tray. It was like travelling in a temple.

The car for sale in Bath was very different: trim and black and without any luxuries inside. The inevitable rust on the front wheel arches was evident as a kind of acne, but it was smartly painted, and I didn't know a lot about such things. I was twenty-two and badly wanted a car, and £80 didn't seem a huge amount – although I am sobered by checking the changing value of the pound and discovering that it would be about £750 in 2008. So I paid the retired railwayman who was selling PMV 143 and drove straight off, managing both the bends and the plunge back down to the valley bottom safely.

I had belatedly joined a huge extended family of Morris Minor owners. Second-hand models were popular among students, and I could identify the sound of the clunky doors and farting exhaust as naturally as I could identify a blackbird's squawk. My first cousins in Bristol had shared an old Moggy saloon and made an unexpected small fortune out of its sale. A couple knocked on their door in a street in Clifton, where the car was parked outside, and offered twice its value (like most of the Minors we knew, it was rust-dappled and the engine knocked). The couple didn't care, because they wanted not the car but its numberplate, DAD 59, for a parental birthday. My cousins sold on the spot, and it was one of those happy deals where everyone ends up content.

By the time my generation achieved seventeen and the right to a provisional licence, the Minor was fighting off its cliché reputation as the choice of vicars and little old ladies who peeped at the road ahead through the space between the dashboard and the top of the steering wheel. We knew about that sort of driver, though; indeed I played a small part in giving one little old lady an exciting surprise by helping to carry her Minor bodily for fifty yards. Once a year the whole of my school took part in a mass run for some four miles through the local suburbs, and the lady's car was caught up in the huge throng. On the spur of the moment, six burly sixth-formers seized the chassis and lifted the Minor off the ground. A stream of us smaller fry grabbed any spare handhold and the car accelerated away on boy power. The elderly lady enjoyed it greatly and thanked us when the car was gently lowered back on to its wheels.

But no. We are not talking Old Banger but *The Love Bug*, the Disney movie about a match-making car, which grossed more takings than any other film when it premiered in 1969. While I was Triumph Heralding and giving illegal pillion rides, a girl from London called Penny Cartledge worked her way through a succession of cheap but stylish cars. She started with one of the Minor's antecedents, the Fiat Topolino or 'Little Mouse'. This is a sweet-looking thing and since Penny was too, she was stopped on several occasions by the police on her way to Exeter University. Their reasons were usually spurious – vague suggestions that a tyre might be worn or an indicator light a little wonky. What they really wanted was to chat up a girl and see what on earth it was that she was driving. Topolinos were big in Italy but very rare in Devon in the late 1960s, and there was much of interest for a mechanically-minded policeman below the bonnet. The feature Penny most liked, for its functional simplicity, was the simple feed of petrol to the engine by gravity from the tank, which was above and behind it.

The Topolino was a relatively expensive car for a student

to run, however, and it soon gave way to a Morris Minor; but not just any old model. Penny had the swish version, the convertible, which made a virtue of Minors' general tendency to let in the air through cracks and not-quite perfect seams. After a bit of wrestling and tugging the whole canvas roof folded back, and you had something vaguely like the Spitfires and MGBs which belonged to better-off students. It was a little more matronly but safer and robust. In the swinging Sixties it also had style, and Penny's went on to a distinguished film career. She sold it in the run-up to her final exams to a props company. Soon afterwards, she spotted its familiar numberplate in the comedy series *Man About the House*, which went down a storm between 1973 and 1976. Minor 9480 MP co-starring with Richard Sullivan, Paula Wilcox and Sally Thomsett – imagine!

So then came UMU 431F, one of the duck-egg blue Minor 1000s – officially Smoke Grey – which seemed at one time to have driven all other colours out of the Cowley paintshop. This particular one was a classic of its type, well-made, well-maintained by previous loving owners, solid and sturdy. It was so solid that when Penny locked herself out of it in Fulham, it resisted all attempts to break into it as firmly as a mediaeval castle. It wasn't until a policeman came along, took a steel comb from his back pocket and did something which I cannot reveal here for security reasons, that we were able to use UMU 431F again.

I say 'we' because by this time Penny and I were an item, and the Smoke Grey Minor was the third party in our lives. It didn't bring us together; we weren't fellow members of a Morris Minor Club. But I think we were both reassured by the other's choice of car. In due course I moved out of the dilapidated flat in Maida Vale which I had on a fixed rent from the Church Commissioners, provided a postal order for 4s 6d a week was paid in the name of Dr David Rawlings. There was just room for us both in Penny's tiny flat in Fulham, which she actually owned. Then I moved into her car, where there was room for us both too. As Spring rain plink-plonked on its roof in the market square of Masham in the Yorkshire Dales, I leaned carefully over the gearstick and asked Penny to marry me. She leaned carefully towards me the other way and said Yes. Had the occasion been directed by Walt Disney, one of UMU 431F's chrome eyelids would have dipped in a wink.

It was just as well that this didn't happen in PMV 143, which we had sold as part of these romantic arrangements. The gearstick obstacle there was compounded by a domestic blow-heater that my ex-railwayman vendor had welded and wired into the front footwell. This was typical of modifications made to Minors of that era, which left the factory with interiors reminiscent of wartime jeeps. By the time PMV 143 went to her new owner, fortunately an enthusiastic restorer, she also had sections of front floor pocked with rust-holes which looked like a bone with osteoporosis. In wet weather such as the day of our engagement (although the sun came out after celebration Brown Windsor soup, roast beef and apple crumble at the King's Head in Masham), this would have created a primitive, cold-water foot spa.

This threesome – Pen, me and the Minor – would have pleased Professor Colin Buchanan, the celebrated author of the 1963 report *Traffic in Towns*, who included the romantic side of car ownership in his thorough but enjoyable survey of the rise of the motor vehicle, *Mixed Blessing*, published in 1958. Much of this consists of dense statistics and tables, but Buchanan also passes on anecdotes including an overheard put-down by a young woman of a boyfriend who claimed to be an eligible bachelor. That would not be the case until he bought a car, she said tartly. Buchanan notes: 'Certainly in the middle classes, the car has become an important part of courtship equipment.'

Was – is – the Moggy particularly suited to this? They certainly thought so at Morris Motors and then BMC, especially when the long-awaited 948cc engine was fitted to the new Minor 1000 in 1956. Testosterone time, but in a cosy way. Now you could steam off from the lights and manage 70 mph relatively comfortably, while young women didn't think they were in the hands of a madman who would drive them to an early grave. An advertisement film for the new model summed the approach up neatly – a dainty girl getting into a Minor 1000 to an elegant if slightly complicated voiceover: 'His sort of motoring in her sort of car. How nice that the sort of car he wanted was the sort she wanted him to want.'

Can we go further, and argue that the Minor's feminine curves and masculine sturdiness create a combination which appeals to, and can even actually stir, both sexes? It is hardly an erotic car, for all that 'Morris Minor' is post-war

Cockney rhyming slang for vagina. The nearest I have come to some sort of anthropomorphic feelings was when I visited Charles Ware's Morris Minor centre in Bristol for the first time and stood in the workshop amid more than forty Moggies, both whole and in bits. They did remind me of something vaguely erotic. What was it? That impression of curves everywhere, of smooth rounded surfaces, of gentle mounds. A painting? Ah yes, *Les Grandes Baigneuses* by Cézanne. Two months later, the thought came back when I stood beside Sue Akrill, Chairman of the Bridlington & Wolds Morris Minor Owners' Club, at a rally in Yorkshire; she looked at a row of the cars and burst out, 'Couldn't you just *stroke* them?' *Les Grandes Baigneuses* swam back into my mind, and I agreed that you just could. Less erotically, another lifelong Morris Minor couple confided on the same occasion that they had always loved the car because of its resemblance to a jelly mould (a view shared by the Morris Minor Owners' Club, the homepage of whose website calls the cars 'lovable jelly moulds'.) The way to a man's heart . . . Many partnerships have been built on the secure foundation of an ability to make and enjoy comfort food, and it is easy to see the appeal of travelling in a car that is a reminder of that.

By now I had discovered a lot about the car's history, and decided with some excitement that it was the product of a love affair itself. Not one between people, which are commonplace, but the rarer sort of a brilliant individual sublimating all his energy and emotion into an idea. The Minor's creator was brilliant indeed, Sir Alec Issigonis, the only car designer in the world whose name is known widely outside enthusiasts' ranks. He was technically masterful, perhaps a genius, but he also had an exceptional understanding of British myth-making, the iconography of teapots and telephone kiosks which the Morris Minor was to join – because he was swathed in it at an early age while at the same time kept safely immune from the real, and much more humdrum, thing.

Issigonis was born not in Surrey but Smyrna, now usually called Izmir and the third largest city in Turkey. He is often referred to as a foreigner, a Turk or a Greek, in thumbnail sketches of his life. Most notoriously, Lord Nuffield described him as 'Issi-wassi-what's his bloody name?' and 'That foreign chap', but all such descriptions were wrong. He was the British son of a British father and British grandfather. But that description is inadequate too: Issigonis's true nationality was More British than the British. He was one of those distant foster-children of the Empire, raised on an ideal of the mother country that was credible only to those who never or seldom went there. I recently heard a talk by Lord Dholakia, the Liberal Democrat home affairs spokesman in the House of Lords, who arrived at Tilbury in the late 1950s as a young student with all these illusions. He expected a warm welcome and thought he would make a good impression if he walked off the ship from Dar-es-Salaam wearing a bowler hat.

Issigonis's family had Greek origins but became Levantines, members of the cosmopolitan community of the Eastern Mediterranean that was encouraged by the decaying but socially tolerant Ottoman empire and famous for producing many outstanding businessmen and engineers. By the time Alexander Arnold Constantine was born in 1906, the Issigonises were running a rich and thriving marine engineering works developed by Alec's grandfather, who had been given British citizenship in the 1870s in return for supporting one of the Victorians' international railway schemes. The little boy was surrounded from the start by the bits, pieces and terminology of engineering, with the factory an occasional playground, and all in the atmosphere of an 'English home', which was actually copied from models such as the *Illustrated London News*. He was Alec, not the more usual Greek Alex; he had an English governess; and his best friend was Donald Riddle, an English boy whose father worked in Smyrna. Together they devoured imported copies of *Boys' Own* magazine. His favourite first cousin, May Walker, was the grand-daughter of a Derbyshire man who had gone to Smyrna to work on new Ottoman railways in the 1860s. Had war not broken out in 1914, and had Turkey not joined the 'wrong' side through an alliance with Germany and Austro-Hungary, Alec would have gone to Oundle public school in Lincolnshire. His father had put him down for a place some years before, as a proper upper-middle-class Englishman should.

These attributes all came together in the form of Meccano, the toy engineering kit that Issigonis used for his very first designs. When the idyll of his childhood collapsed in terrible circumstances in 1922, the year the disastrous Greek invasion of Turkey ended with the sacking of

Smyrna, he was allowed to accompany his father on a brief and dangerous return to the city to collect a few extra possessions before returning to one of the Royal Navy warships which evacuated British citizens. He came back on board with his precious Meccano, and the family went first to Malta and then to London, where he soon realised that the fond hopes for his upbringing were wide of the mark. He was a refugee from an exotic but mistrusted part of the world, with a funny name and a German mother (Mrs Issigonis's family moved from Stuttgart to Smyrna in the 1840s to start a brewery). However assiduously he ate marmalade and did the *Daily Telegraph* crossword every day, both lifelong habits, he would never entirely fit in.

This did not make life easy, as Issigonis struggled with engineering studies in his chilly new homeland and much reduced circumstances (his father had died in Malta), but it was important to his design genius. Like the first experimenters with marmalade (which originally came from Spain) or the archetypal English bungalow (actually from India), he naturally looked outwards for new ideas in a way that conventional young Englishmen raised in Britain were less likely to do. This was to come to fruition in the Morris Minor. Its marvellous suspension owed something to Issigonis's careful study of experiments by Continental car firms. Its body shape, so soon to become iconically 'English', was the product of what Issigonis called his American period. He spent hours poring over streamlined American fridges, irons, railway engines and, of course, cars: late 1930s and early 1940s Buicks, Cadillacs, Chevrolets and Pontiacs.

Everything was bulbous and rounded from new pressed-steel and die-casting methods. The watchwords were aerodynamic, sheer, flush and clean.

Watch an American gangster film from this period, and you are in a world of oversized Minors, cars like the 1939 Ford V8 'Woodie', which has the look of an obese Morris Traveller, or the Oldsmobile range of early 1940s saloons whose bustle boot, domed bonnet and outward-curving doorsills are Brobdingnagian versions of the very same features on a Minor. America's love affair with huge, tail-finned beasts in the 1950s blinded my generation to this influence, which at the time was an extraordinary transformation from the boxy, straight lines of most European cars. American? Our little Moggy? If you still have doubts, look at a Morris Minor front door and compare it with the recent retro marque boldly produced by Chrysler, the PT Cruiser. They are so alike, you could swap them.

There was something else about Issigonis which was added to this rich mix, and which adds to my belief that the Morris Minor is a love child. Issigonis never married and had no family, and, although he was a devoted son to his mother and a wonderful uncle, he had no known outlet for the sexual drive which is all but universal among human beings. He had some mannerisms which today would be called camp, such as using the term 'My dear' to men as well as women, and his friends included gay men. But those were very different times from today. Issigonis's crucial patron Sir Miles Thomas, who forced the Minor into production against opposition from Nuffield, loses all his geniality when he discusses homosexuality briefly in his autobiography *Out on a Wing*, which was published in 1964. 'Until this very day, I do not know the mechanics of the practice,' he writes, continuing floridly: 'Revelling in its freedom as a snake relishes a warm, moist, insect-strewn midden, it became fashionable among queer-minded fellows who, had they been kept in ignorance, would not have had the enterprise to ferret things out for themselves.'

It is hardly surprising that Issigonis's assiduous biographer Gillian Bardsley, who examined his life exceptionally diligently during the nine years she spent preparing her book, found no evidence that he was gay. She echoes contemporaries who were sure that his work was his life. He had great and lasting friendships with men and women, but he appears not have wanted the burden of close relationships or the pram in the hall which Cyril Connolly describes as the 'enemy of promise'. John Cooper, who worked with Issigonis on the Mini Cooper, says simply: 'He was married to motor cars. His whole life was motor cars. Day and night he'd talk about motor cars. He didn't talk about other things.' I would respectfully adjust this slightly. He was married to motor car design. The cars themselves were his children, and the Minor was the firstborn.

As such, it gave him plenty of problems. Anyone familiar with a Moggy knows how they can misbehave, give a love bite or just kick out. My colleague at the *Guardian*, Lisa Darnell, has a very slight scar behind her left ear which was caused by her mother's Morris Minor. Lisa was four at the time and, as she told me with feeling, 'it was the era when you didn't have to wear seatbelts. In fact you didn't even have to sit down.' Little Lisa was therefore standing on the front passenger seat when her mother had to brake sharply, and she flew forward and clocked the side of her head on the Minor's distinctive door handle at dashboard height. 'There was loads of blood but we were just near Wellingborough cottage hospital,' she said. 'They cleaned me up but couldn't do the main stuff – careful stitching – so we had to go to Kettering.' The detail she remembers is that they also had to find a faster car to get her there.

I never injured myself or anyone else in my Minor career, although Penny had one, similar, sharp braking episode through no fault of her own, which briefly left a student passenger with Botox lips from hitting the dash. But I was lucky. On a sunny day, in a happy mood, I was bowling down the Leeds ring road from Owlcotes to Rodley when suddenly everything went black. It was my most terrifying moment in thirty years of driving. I thought I had suffered a heart attack or brain haemorrhage, or somehow hit something enormous without there being any noise. How you have so many thoughts in what must be fractions of a second, I don't know; but they were ended by a hideous screech of tearing metal and the sky reappeared.

I had instinctively swung on to the verge and braked drastically, and it was just as well. The black was the top of PMV 143's bonnet, which I had clearly not secured when checking the oil earlier in the day. A huge thing, designed to swing back and up on its hinges when the engine needed inspecting, it had bounced up just enough to catch the slipstream like a clipper sail. One hinge simply ripped away – I was doing 60 mph – but miraculously the other held. The bonnet finished up on the Minor's roof which it scored like a knife, but stayed clamped to the left hand wing by the hinge's twisted arm. No wonder the Morris 1000 workshop manual makes a point about the bonnet lock, emphasising the need to almost slam the thing shut and give it a couple of pushes and pulls to check that everything is secure. I sure did feel stupid – albeit extremely relieved. There had been a line of cars behind me, and a flying, 60-mph bonnet could have done dreadful damage.

Many years later, however, I read Gillian Bardsley's account of a similar episode involving Issigonis himself, which made me feel that I was in good company. Between the Minor and the Mini, Issigonis had a spell at Alvis, where he designed one of the great modern British cars which was never made, the TA350 four-door saloon with a 3.5-litre V8 engine. It proved too expensive for a small, specialist car company, but got as far as a prototype which was hurled round the Motor Industry Research Association's high-speed test circuit at Lindley, near Nuneaton, at speeds of up to 110 mph. Lapping furiously on one occasion in 1954, Issigonis's co-driver Harry Barber, Alvis's chief body engineer, suddenly had exactly the same blackout experience as mine – and for the same reason. The bonnet reared up in the air, hung for a flash and then tore completely loose, walloping the roof and leaving a deep dent before flying off behind the car on to a fortunately empty track. After that the prototype was fitted with leather straps to back up the bonnet lock, and those involved never forgot the episode. When Issigonis was knighted in 1969 Barber wrote a letter of congratulation which recalled the happy old days of 'bonnets flying through the air'.

I also noticed, when I came to inspect the millionth Morris Minor to be made, as described in Chapter Four, that its bonnet looked suspiciously loose. I mentioned this, and the car's loving owner rolled his eyes, before we shared disapproving opinions of this flaw in our otherwise lovable cars. Note, too, the tragic picture on the back flap of this book. That is what happens when a trunnion goes. I have less reason to escape blame for this, because the trunnions of a Minor do not have the problematic slight dodginess of the bonnet catch. The workshop manual says that when they do go, it is usually the result of a lack of regular maintenance.

I confess. I had never heard of a trunnion at the time; I didn't even know what one was, let alone how to ensure it was properly maintained. Penny and I did get UMU 431F repaired after that episode however, even though the caption to the picture in our photograph album records that 'various shady people made us offers for the car'. It was one of the only occasions that either of our Morris Minors let us down, and the trunnion did at least manage to keep going to within a ten-minute sprint of Penny's Fulham flat. (This was crucial, because we were due to meet an Army officer there who subsequently made an offer on the flat, which Penny accepted and which allowed us to buy a terraced house in Chiswick together and so start respectably on married life.)

We did not involve UMU in our big day, however: a shame in retrospect, because Penny's big hired limo was held up on the way to the church by the changing of the guard at Buckingham Palace. A picture of a Morris Minor with white ribbons waiting for the redcoats in busbies would have been a nice souvenir for the tourists as well as ourselves. We drove around in UMU every ordinary day, but this was not an ordinary day; there would have been nothing special about going to our ceremony in a Morris Minor. Goodness, how *that* has changed.

The love child of a genius. A Cézanne nude made metal. Now, I discovered, as I met Minor after Minor while writing this book, the car has become as totemic of the modern British wedding as the cake and posy tossed to guests for the next nubile young woman to catch. Car after car has been used to take a bride to her groom, or booked to do so, from Tony Manos's heroic Moggy just back from Ulan Bator (see Chapter 9) to Max the Saloon and Milo the Traveller fighting for the honour in the children's book *Meet the Moggies*, where a wedding disrupts life in Mr Grubby's garage. Above all, there was Gladys, whose smile and lidded headlamps pouted out at me from an advertising postcard on the wall at Charles Ware's Morris Minor centre. She promised 'to add glamour and style to your wedding day', adding coyly: 'with the top down and the sun out, you will certainly enjoy the ride'.

Gladys the Wedding Car lives in Dorset and had always had women owners until Guy Gilding decided to pay for her restoration by hiring her out for other couples' happiest days. The omens weren't specially good; times had been difficult for him after a divorce so acrimonious that he set up a website encouraging others to describe the horrors of their ex-partners, satirical but with evident feeling behind it. Still, Gladys was an excellent way of cheering himself up.

'You have a nice drive to collect people who are pleased to see you; they're excited on the journey; they come out of the church even happier than before; and you have another nice drive to take them away. It's just a day of happiness,' he says. For his clients, arrival and departure in a Morris Minor is the icing on the cake. They are almost always fans specifically of the Minor, rather than people who want a classic or funky car regardless of the make.

Gladys went to the Bournemouth wedding fair this year, and it was an instructive experience. Parked between a Rolls Royce and a horse-drawn carriage, she got Guy three bookings, all from couples who wanted a Morris Minor and nothing else. Across the way was a VW Kombi camper van, the type used by young Australians to tour Europe before getting sold on to other travellers at informal street markets in central London:

They were much busier – ended up with nineteen bookings. But not from people who had a passion for VWs or camper vans; it was just a fun thing. Our people really, really want a Minor.

He likes it that way.

The car was made in 1961 and bought for Guy's mother in Christchurch by his father who was an inveterate haggler. 'He got the price down to £130.01 but the seller wouldn't budge from that. Not even over the penny.' Gladys hadn't been about much; her registration 1623 LJ was a Bournemouth one, and she pootled decorously around Dorset with Guy's mum. Her most exotic travels were to Kent, when Guy's sister went to work there and took Gladys with her, eventually running the car into the ground. Gladys spent two years in a garage before Guy rescued her for his then wife, taking the car to Charles Ware's to get her fit for the road.

But Gladys continued to get run into the ground, among other things. 'She got reversed out of the garage with one of her doors open, which was a mistake.' It was too much, and seven years in mothballs followed, until a big clearout at the time of the divorce.

I had to decide: do I scrap Gladys or keep her. I couldn't bear the thought of scrapping, even though she was in a real mess. So I took out a loan to do her up, hiring her out for the weddings to pay the money back.

Guy also had Gladys turned into a convertible, a common practice in modern conversions of Minors, with the bodywork strengthened and cannibalised parts from scrapyard cars used for the hood with its notorious butterfly clips. 'OK, purists will scream and say that we've committed sacrilege,' says Guy. 'But everything under the bonnet is original, including genuine mushy Morris Minor brakes.' These have held up to now, conveying half-a-dozen brides and grooms safely in the business's first year, although there have been other hazards in Gladys's forty-seven-year life. As Guy waited outside one North Dorset church to chauffeur the couple to their reception, the bell-ringers who had come over to admire the car noticed that one of its tyres was gently going down. Guy had forgotten the jack, but a ringer – also a Moggy owner, dashed home to get his – and together the group of them just managed to change the wheel before the bells rang and the couple emerged from the church.

They would probably have been delighted by such a typical piece of Minor behaviour. Guy has had several brides and grooms who settled back as the engine started running with a contented sigh of: 'Just listen to that wonderful noise.' The general atmosphere of joy is often supplemented by passers-by coming up and saying, 'Aaaah, my first car was a Morris Minor,' just as I did at the beginning of this chapter, or 'I taught my kids to drive in one of these.' Even the fuel pump gets some clients going: turn the ignition and you get a faint tick-tick-tick as it pushes through some petrol before ignition starts. 'Actually the fuel pump is Gladys's least reliable point but I know what to do if it stops,' says Guy. 'Lift the bonnet and tap the pump with something sturdy.' It's a ceremony that has yet to happen in front of a wedding couple, but Guy is sure they would consider it part of the Minor experience if it did.

Gladys has much less room than a Rolls Royce or horse-drawn carriage – or VW Kombi – but the Minor's simple interior works well for brides. Guy usually seats them in the back with the front passenger seat folded horizontal and flat. 'If the top's down – which it usually is for a summer wedding – they can literally step inside.' It took me back to Fulham days with UMU, after a broken leg ended my motorcycling career. We took out the front passenger seat altogether and I sat in the back like royalty with my leg – plastered up to the hip – stretched out straight in front of me.

I also thought of *The Love Bug* again. If only a bigger engine and more punchy marketing had been used for the Minor in the United States in the 1950s, Herbie the VW Beetle that starred in the film and its six sequels (the most recent, *Herbie – Full Loaded*, as recently as 2005) plus a TV series, might have been Moggy the Minor. It would have had the same effect as *The Italian Job* did on the fame of the Mini, only much greater. Just imagine where my favourite car would stand in world opinion now! And, come to think of it, where *does* it stand in Britain today? My next job was to find out.

Chapter 2
Minor Meetings

There has never been a bad Morris Minor.

Motor magazine, 1956

I TURNED FIFTY-EIGHT THIS YEAR – two years younger than the Morris Minor – and, although I continue to feel like a twenty-year-old, I appreciate that the world has changed. This struck me when I started to research this book, and it was a lesson repeated when I encountered cars such as Gladys the Wedding Minor. To some extent, I still live inside my head in a world where Morris Minors are part of the everyday roadscape, as they were when I was genuinely just out of my teens. How common are they really now, today, in 2008?

I decided to observe in a scientific way, keeping a record in a pocket notebook of every Morris Minor I met. It was easy through Google to discover that statistically there are reckoned to be 30,000 still running in Britain, but is that reflected on the roads? I started looking at the beginning of January, and by the end of the month I had seen . . . none. Was my project a farce? Would I have to fall back on describing the cars I met at Charlie Ware's factory and later, in April, when I went out on the North York Moors with the Bridlington & Wolds Morris Minor Owners' Club?

I was almost reconciled to that sort of cheating when I had to take my mother and an uncle to a golden wedding in Wiltshire, and we picked up an aunt on the way at Hungerford railway station. The three of us were sitting comfortably in the car, chatting before the aunt's train from Paddington arrived, when I saw an unmistakable, sweetly rounded shape tuck into a parking space. It was a Morris Minor at last, and not just any old Morris Minor but a convertible apparently made in heaven. Its condition was immaculate and its livery a beautiful and clearly bespoke combination of buttermilk cream and a dark, viridian green.

Inside was a friendly financier from London called Charles Hansard, and there was a bundle of appetising lunchtime shopping on the back seat plus an orchid in a pot. I caught the scent of leather and there seemed to be a particularly fine carpet. I apologised for being nosey, but cars like this seldom get away without attracting rubberneckers and Mr Hansard was courteous and happy to help. 'It's actually my wife's car,' he explained, 'and these are colours which she often recommends to clients of her interior decorating business.' Soon after, I was enjoying the website of Joanna Wood and then chatting to Ms Wood herself.

'I'd always liked them,' she said.

My PA had a lovely one, and there came a time when I was fed up with either my husband or someone in the office borrowing my car, so I thought: I'll get one which nobody wants to nick.

She checked trade adverts and bought a 1955 Minor unseen from a vicar in Leicestershire. Excellent. The first on my list of sightings conformed to traditional type. But not for long. Joanna sent it away to Charlie Ware to have a boot-to-bonnet restoration, and it came back not just with its pristine looks but with a Chevrolet gearbox and powerful Cortina engine as well. 'People get quite surprised when you razz it up at traffic lights and steam away on green.' She's got used to twenty-year-olds coming up to her and saying 'Cool car.' At the other end of the spectrum, what she calls '120-year-olds' potter by misty-eyed and say: 'I remember them.'

The car's carpets are indeed snazzy. Joanna had them made up specially by a friend at Hugh Mackay, the Axminster specialist whose carpets also cover floors at the Houses of Parliament and Windsor Castle. She also compares notes with another friend from the world of interior decoration, David Linley, the furniture designer and son of Lord Snowdon and Princess Margaret. 'He has a lovely Morris Minor in black, red and cream,' she says. 'He's been keeping it at his house in France, but we swap anecdotes.' As for Ms Wood, her car tends to make only gentle journeys round Wiltshire these days, occasionally refusing to start. 'We use it for things like meeting trains at Hungerford railway station,' she said. 'Once we've got going, it has never let me down.'

I decided to add the semi-royal Linley car to my note-book as sighting number two, reflecting on the fact that a master of woodwork had gone for a convertible rather than a Traveller. Maybe that is to come. This change of policy came just in time, because my next meeting was also not literally with a Morris Minor but with a former owner of three of them: a saloon, a Traveller and – relatively unusually – a van. Bridget Johnson was next to me in the queue to get on to the Bristol-bound train at Birmingham New Street when I was on my way to see the photographer Martin Parr to talk about his pictures of abandoned Morris Minors in the West of Ireland. The electronic reservation signs were not working, and there was a certain amount of milling about and confusion before we settled down correctly, Bridget by the window in 33W and me by the aisle in 34A. So we got chatting, then we both worked for a bit and then we both wanted a coffee at the same time and so we got chatting again and my mission emerged. 'Oh, we used to have Morris Minors,' said Bridget in a fond way that was by now familiar. And then (as I could have predicted): 'I can tell you a tale or two about them.' And she did.

The first involved the family's Traveller and a primary school project, when one of her four children was asked to bring a fungus for the class's nature table. Central Stoke-on-Trent, where the Johnsons were living, wasn't blessed with toadstools but Bridget and her husband Tony knew where to find some. 'A little colony of them grew on the Traveller between the wooden struts and the windows where it was always damp,' she said. The children scraped samples off, and they went down a storm. 'What type were they? What were they called?' I wondered. 'Come on!' she said. 'This was only primary school!'

The Johnson children also played an important role on journeys to school in the van, a properly workaday vehicle like a mobile allotment shed, whose sides had a habit of bulging out and so were fixed together with rope, in the manner of a tie-beam through an old house. This caused delays when Bridget was loading the van with clay slip for her work at the time as a potter, as the heavy bags had to be hoicked over the rope or slid underneath it. But when the children piled in the back on a heap of cushions, it was useful to grab on corners. This was before the days of safety belts. Anyway, one of the four had to be handy to jump out quickly, because the van had an intermittent fuel pump problem, which could only be solved by sharp knocks.

> We kept a cricket stump in the van, and when we stopped, which could happen three times just on the short journey to school, I slipped the bonnet release, the chosen child nipped out, did the catch and gave the pump a series of whacks. It always worked.

Bridget was a mine of information, and not just on Morris Minors. I had no idea that an early edition of the VW Golf suffered from gradual rusting of the metal cap on the fuel intake, so that tiny flakes gradually starved the engine of petrol. The Johnsons puzzled this out from a German manual which came with their model, a right-hand drive car built in Germany for a British army officer. (They got it after finally moving on from the Morris Minors, a heady period which also saw the children stylishly conveyed to school in an old Daimler, until its brakes and steering failed simultaneously, luckily without hurting anyone.) But Bridget remains an authority on Minors, picking me up when I referred to one I'd met as being 'a sort of creamy colour'. ('Snowberry, you mean! Ours was Snowberry.') Their Traveller, however, was a sort of grey unknown to the Morris paintshop at Cowley, and the Johnson van was resplendent in gloss green salvaged from Tony's former job at one of Stoke's famous potteries. He and Bridget did the whole job by hand and thereafter considered the vehicle to have been carriage-painted.

When the train pulled into Temple Meads, Bridget had to scoot off to get a taxi to the nursing home where her mother was recovering from pneumonia. I wandered over to the stop for the Zoo bus which used to take us up to Clifton where my cousins lived, the ones who sold the Morris Minor for its DAD 59 number plate. It wasn't a huge loss for them because their parents had one of those wonderful old Humbers which swallowed you in leather upholstery — probably the most comfortable car I've ever travelled in, certainly as a child. A number 9 bus was waiting but the bus company man said that it wasn't going for quarter of an hour, which would have cut it fine with Martin Parr. So I went back to the taxi rank and sailed off into the Bristol traffic.

The driver quickly discovered why I was in Bristol and

was pleased about it. 'Morris Minor?' he said. 'Everywhere in Pakistan. Easy to look after; do pretty much all the repairing yourself. That's a car that lasts a long, long time.' We got on to his family, four children all now qualified medics, after university respectively at Oxford, Cambridge, London and Edinburgh. I was busy paying compliments when he whooped out 'Morris Minor, sir!', and there among the cars parked along Cornwallis Crescent was a duck-egg blue saloon. There wasn't a chance to leave one of my notes under the windscreen wipers because the driver was intent on getting me to Martin's in time for my appointment, so we zoomed on past.

The next Minor meeting was also high-speed and with no chance for anything but a beam and a wave. En route to a friend's sixtieth birthday party in Salisbury, we passed a crack-condition Minor van being ferried down the M1 in state on a trailer; maybe on its way to a rally somewhere near Northampton, where it turned off. Penny was specially pleased. 'That's the Rose Taupe I've been on about,' she said. I had read about it and Googled a picture, but this was the first I'd actually seen in the pinky, moleskinny colour ('taupe' being French for 'mole').

And then, on the wall in the undercroft at Salisbury Cathedral choir school, there was the next sighting: a child's pencil sketch of a Minor looking a bit groggy but still on all four wheels. I'd been discussing Morris Minors with some of the other guests, gently so as not to appear obsessed, and since we were pretty much all of an age, half-a-dozen of them turned out to have owned second-, third- or more-hand Minors in their student days. We gathered round the drawing murmuring approval of the young artist's picture. They'd really got the sense of the car, the friendliness, the anthropomorphic face. When I was back in Leeds, I got in touch with the school to ask who had drawn it and why.

'It was fabulous. It was thanks to Gillian Bathe, our art teacher,' said a cheery voice at the other end.

> One of the parents has a Morris Minor, and they brought it in for the children to sketch. They loved it. They did all different angles, some from far away, some really detailed. It was one of the best exercises of that sort that the school's had.

Excellent. Minors might be scarcer than I hoped, but they weren't appealing just to fogeys of my age. Mrs Bathe let all 250 kids in the school, from three- to thirteen-year-olds, have a look at the car, and the overwhelming response was: Aaaah.

Back in Leeds, I surveyed the roads daily, with their everyday lines of oval modern saloons, boxy people-carriers and brutish pretend-Jeeps. Nary a familiar rounded top. How rare the old Moggy had become. And then – as I drove down Tinshill Road in Cookridge, after interviewing the Environment Secretary Hilary Benn in a carbon-saving 'house of the future' on nearby Green Lane – an absolute beauty, a dark blue convertible, turned out of Hillcrest Drive. This is a steep little hill where we used to go to post letters from the house on Tinshill Road where I was born. It is also famous in the family for an episode on our daily walk back from primary school, when we saw a mole surface in the field which then flanked the road, and a woman waiting at the bus stop told us it was a baby cow. A memorable spot to meet a Minor so many years later! But before I could catch the driver's eye, it showed a clean pair of heels and shot off down towards Horsforth railway station. Should I flash it? There was rather a lot of traffic tanking along in the opposite direction, and the usual slow-up where shoppers park before the Old Ball roundabout for once didn't happen. I lost him.

More disappointment followed. In town two weeks later a beige Morris Minor saloon was parked beside the Henry Moore Institute. It didn't seem to be part of one of their challenging exhibitions, and I stuck a note under the wipers with my 'phone number and a brief explanation of my Minor-hunting quest. It apparently wasn't eloquent enough because nobody rang (although I noticed that the car was in a disabled parking bay, so its owner may have thought that I was part of the traffic wardens' ever more cunning – and justified – methods of imposing the law).

Disconsolate after a week with no response from the Henry Moore Minor, I turned on the TV one evening and found a documentary about my famous namesake, the fell walker Alfred Wainwright, under way. It was one of many repeats of the programme, and I had a personal interest because the producer, Eric Harwood, had got me to write a BBC book to go with the series when it first appeared in the summer of 2007. I watched with half an eye but then sat up straight as – guess what – a fine old green Morris Minor trundled into the centre of the screen, and the actor playing Wainwright uncrumpled his six-feet-plus and got out. Just a minute, I thought. I remembered this episode very well from Hunter Davies's biography, because it was a momentous step for the cautious and conservative A.W. He had always previously taken buses. But the love of his life, Betty McNally, who gave him happiness after a disastrous first marriage, finally persuaded him to accept her offer of lifts. Their romance was clandestine but word got out, and Wainwright's wife was told by friends that something was going on with 'a woman in a Mini'. But it wasn't a Mini (and it wasn't a Minor either). Betty had a VW Beetle.

I emailed Eric out of interest; not because it was a significant issue (although Wainwright himself was fastidious over detail) but because I sensed what Eric was likely to say. And he did. The car was wrong because the TV team could not source a Beetle of the right period in the Lakes in the limited time they had. But, in Eric's words, 'It was strange how many people felt that a Morris Minor was just right.' More right, indeed, than a Beetle. His assistant Philippa Page, who was handling the emails at his end, also chipped in. 'I love Morris Minors,' she wrote. When she was five or six, her Mum had an eggshell blue Traveller, and she had a great time stirring the puddles in the footwell when it rained, and using her fingernails to scrape moss off the wood, like Bridget Johnson's children and their fungus. She fell for a maroon convertible when she was twenty-one and too poor to afford it, and missed out again when she was working in the Western Isles on the BBC TV series *Castaway*. She swore that she would reward herself for the long, cold and isolated days by getting a Minor at last when filming was over. But the BBC posted her to London, where it was too expensive to keep a car. 'I still live in hope,' she said. 'In the meantime I can just admire them. I saw a beautiful one last week driving through Bridport, with a split screen, immaculate condition – Poop! Poop!' I decided that it would be fair to add that one, and the Wainwright film car, to my faltering list.

Events then led to a meeting with renowned London bagpiper Stuart Murray and his wife Carol, or Bunny. Bunny had looked out of her bedroom window some years before, after a discussion with Stuart on her inability to drive. Below in the street was parked a Traveller, all friendliness and curves as ever, and Bunny called Stuart over and said: 'That's the car I'd like to learn to drive in.' 'That's lucky,' he replied, 'because I bought it for you yesterday.' The gift proved an inspiration. Nicknamed 'the Bumpy Car' by the Murrays' growing family, it got Bunny through the test and conveyed their three children round London for years. 'It did what it said on the tin,' says Bunny, who is no more likely to want to look under a car bonnet than I am. 'It had four wheels, and it started when you turned the starter thing.' The only anxious moments were when the Traveller, with Bunny at the helm, embarked on the rapids of the Shepherd's Bush roundabout near their home. The Murrays' small daughter Holly had accompanied her mother on driving lessons and picked up Stuart's urgent shouts of 'Go!' As the Traveller nosed out of Shepherd's Bush Road, Holly would command 'Go!' in the same tone, and Bunny would oblige. The 'Morris Minor effect' of disarming all but the most impatient drivers always saw them safely through.

The Bumpy Car might have been a little primitive for the 1980s in its seating comfort and suspension, but it could put on a brisk turn of speed. One night Bunny answered the phone after 2 a.m. and it was the police asking for Stuart. 'What's he done now?' she asked blearily (although Stuart is actually an entirely law-abiding company secretary). 'It's not him, it's his car,' said the police, who had done a handy bit of detective work when they saw the Bumpy Car out after midnight driven by a couple of young men with an empty child seat in the back. This wasn't normal Morris Traveller behaviour, they reasoned, and on went the blue light. Off took the Traveller, which had been stolen from outside the Murrays' home and used to rob a Kentucky Fried Chicken outlet. 'They can go quite fast, those Travellers, can't they?' the officer on duty told Stuart when he arrived to collect the car. The chase had gone round and round Holland Park and Notting Hill for almost half-an-hour. The Bumpy Car was undamaged and indeed, in Bunny's opinion, had probably only benefited from a brief spell of the sort of driving it never normally got in her hands. It was certainly more impressive than a 1961 Minor that featured in *Weekend* magazine in April 1983 because of a misunderstanding over its theft. After it was recovered, police told the owner that the car had been used in a bank robbery.

'Wonderful!' he said. 'To think that a 1961 Moggy was used as a getaway car.'

'You misunderstand,' said the officer. 'It was not used to get away. It was used to block the road.'

Bunny remembered, too, a university friend who threw anti-rust and -fungus caution to the winds with his Traveller by growing African Marigolds in the summer in soil packed into the lip at the sides of the roof. This romantic gesture attracted young women, although the car had disadvantages in that respect. One particularly sought-after date started getting cold on the way back from a party and asked if the heater could be turned on. Thinking quickly, the marigold-grower said 'Of course,' and went through a short pantomime in the dark of flicking switches and turning knobs on the dashboard, which had few of either, while encouraging her to wrap her shawl more tightly round her and to borrow his coat. In accordance with Sir Alec Issigonis's aversion to filling his cars with 'domestic appliances', the Traveller didn't run to a heater.

At the function where Bunny told me this, there was another friend listening, just in his sixties, so I asked him if he had had a Morris Minor too. His two-word answer spoke volumes about the car's incredible penetration of our generation. Looking at me as though I had asked if he had eyes or was wearing shoes, he said simply: 'Of course.'

April arrived, and Penny and I went walking in Farndale's wild daffodil valley with the rally drivers from the Bridlington & Wolds Morris Minors Owners' Club. I raised my concern about the general absence of the car. 'Ah,' said Richard Hall, a fifty-seven-year-old retired engineer from the British Aerospace factory in Brough. 'That's because they're all inside during the winter, because of the salt.' Talking about the cars as though they were flowers like the daffodils, he went on. 'They're not out yet. It's too early in the year. Mine's just come out today for the first time.' So I continued to scan the roads, not just in Leeds but on Tyneside and in Manchester, trying to avoid motorways where possible on the grounds that most Minors by now are more comfortable on A- and B-roads. At last, in May, I spotted the familiar shape turn out of New Adel Lane into Lawnswood Road and accelerate off in the direction of Headingley and Leeds with the familiar farting growl, or what another Moggy driver described to me as 'doing a raspberry in overdrive'. It was the same, beautifully kept convertible that I'd chased unsuccessfully through Horsforth. Once again, I was frustrated, blocked by three cars so I couldn't nip through the forecourt of the Esso garage opposite Lawnswood cemetery and cut him off. 'Next time,' I said out loud, to the surprise of a mother and child on their way to post something in the letterbox. By then, like the White Rabbit in *Alice in Wonderland*, the Minor had scuttled away.

I got a new one, though, two days later, again impossible to stop, but a distinctive specimen in the same blue as our old UMU and with a very large, customised roof rack. I was stuck in the jam on Headingley Lane going into Leeds and he (for again the driver was a man) was enjoying the open road in the opposite direction. And then I struck gold. Penny and I had been to a wedding in Richmond Park, of the daughter of a friend, Pat McGowan, former crime correspondent of the London *Evening Standard*, who in his fifties fulfilled a life's ambition by retraining as a driver for South West Trains. Loyally, we went and came back by SWT, on the line which threads through the suburbs via Clapham Junction. Returning to Waterloo in the gloaming and with plenty of alcohol consumed, I suddenly jerked awake, grabbed Penny and said: 'God! A police car! Is it real?' There was only one other dozy passenger, who gave us a glance as we rattled into Wandsworth Town station, and I wondered if I had been dreaming. But I was absolutely sure that I had seen the once-familiar pale-blue-and-white stripe pattern of a Morris Minor panda car, complete with a rooftop 'taxi bubble' saying Police, in some sort of yard not far from the railway line.

I guessed it must be a film lot or a company which hired out old cars, like the one which bought 9480 MP from Penny when she left university. A fortnight later, I had the chance to truant from work on a visit to London. It cost £3.20 return on SWT and took a couple of hours to do the round trip from King's Cross, with time built in for a little investigation at the Wandsworth end. I stayed on the train past Wandsworth Town and . . . Yes! – there it was: just a shy curve of rear wing and boot peeping out from a row of parked emerald green lorries and vans. A few more of these, or a slightly more disciplined parking system, and the Morris Minor would have been hidden. But now I was on the trail. I backtracked at Putney, saw the car again momentarily, and used my Lake District fell-walking experience – a quick gap in the mist, suss out the landscape and take your bearings – to work out the best way to walk from Wandsworth Town station. Ten minutes later, in boiling sunshine, I was at the deserted gates of Wandsworth Borough Council's Frogmore transport depot.

The yard was slumbering in the heat, the only movement in the sea of green council vehicles coming from a lazy black-and-white cat and two gardeners planting red geraniums in window boxes in front of the office building. Their faces softened when I explained my odd mission and, using the gentle tones everyone seems to adopt when talking about Morris Minors, they said: 'Ah the police car. She's Trevor's. You'll find him over there, that door next to the joiner's shop.' Trevor Critchell, the council's transport manager, was out at a meeting, but his deputy Ricky Cousins was only too pleased to show me the old car. Unlocking a glass-fronted cabinet on the office wall, he picked her keys from rows of bunches hanging on hooks and we pottered over to SYT 671F, or Milly as she has been known for the last fifteen years. 'Milly and Billy – they were a great draw at fairs round here,' he said, explaining that Wandsworth bought the Minor and a flashy old Jaguar XJ6 – Billy – in the mid-1990s as part of a crime prevention programme. Neither cost a lot, although a sticker in Milly's back window proudly proclaims that she took part in the London to Brighton fun run under the banner of the West Sussex Morris Minor Owners' Club. Her role in displays at fairs in the borough, and visits to schools and estates in between, was to be the virtuous Milly, vehicle of the law, while Billy was used by the bad 'uns, actors pretending to be burglars, conmen or drug-dealers who were the target of the campaign. It was – still is, although Billy is no more – an effective harkback to friendly, Dixon of Dock Green policing, with the homely little Minor central to that approach.

Ricky opened Milly's boot, which, like most Minor boots I have known, didn't fit precisely, and fished out a peculiar box from a pile of big signs saying 'Milly', plus the precious starting handle and bundles of crime prevention leaflets. 'I'll show you what this does,' he said, slotting the plywood box, reinforced by sliced up bicycle tyre round its rim, on top of the Police bubble sign on the roof. 'We're not allowed on the road with the Police sign showing unless we've got a real police officer on board,' he said. 'Likewise, we've magnetic metal sheets which cover the Police signs on the passenger doors.' Milly keeps her other window stickers at all times, though: 'Don't give them an easy ride' and 'Crime – lets bring it down.' Inside, the clock reads 87,702, and the sparse little dashboard's only extra is wiring for the council's internal radio network, with an electronic box and phone beneath the glovebox. Ricky slots in the ignition keys and turns them and of course she doesn't start. It turns out she's waiting for minor repairs to a scrape on her nearside rear wing, hit by one of the dozens of green vans during a bad bit of parking.

It is a long time since Milly has seen serious action on a

daily basis, but she had her moment a year ago, as Ricky explained.

The Met discovered her through a local contact, and they've started getting keen on using her for weddings. One of their officers took her for a drive, and on the way back he was alerted to an incident. He told me afterwards: 'When that happens, you've got to go.' So off he roars, in Milly the Morris Minor, with the Police signs showing of course, 'cos with an officer driving, that's OK. When he turned up at whatever it was – some sort of dispute I think, they wouldn't believe he was a real policeman to begin with. 'You don't come in Morris Minors usually,' they said.

It was May now, and Richard Hall's theory about Morris Minors coming out with the good weather was up for testing. Aubretia and Welsh poppies followed the bluebells and tulips into bloom in my garden and, sure enough, those familiar curving bonnets and wheel casings started to appear more frequently. A pale blue Morris sped down Headingley Lane with a big, customised roof rack on top. A Traveller crossed the canal at Apperley Bridge as we waited at the chicane formed by the bridge. A dark blue saloon nudged out of a side turning in Otley on the way to my birthday lunch at Darley in Nidderdale, but then it was gone. And then I went to interview Dr Jeffrey Sherwin, a friend of mine who over the years has amassed the world's largest collection of British Surrealist art at his otherwise ordinary suburban home in Alwoodley, where the road to Harrogate leaves Leeds. Surreally enough, we diverted from art briefly on to the subject of Morris Minors, when Jeffrey explained his first lucky break in the field of buying fine art.

'I'd seen the name of this chap called Bratby,' he said, harking back to the late 1950s when he was at Oxford University. 'I tracked him down to an address in London and went to see him. He tried to get me to buy various pictures which weren't selling, but I stuck out for what I wanted.' Thus Dr Sherwin, a Leeds GP at the time and a prominent Conservative councillor in the city, became one of the first owners of John Bratby's celebrated sunflower studies. He told me how he had anchored three of them down in his convertible Morris Minor – which is when the conversation switched from art to cars. 'You had a Morris Minor?' I asked, over a pile of pictures by Roland Penrose, John Piper and René Magritte which were being bubble-wrapped and crated for an exhibition at the Middlesbrough Institute of Modern Art. 'I certainly did,' said Jeffrey. 'And I drove it to Moscow in 1958.'

The AA had agreed an overland route into the Soviet Union that year for private motorists, he said.

I thought: if the AA can do this in a Land Rover, I can do it in a Morris 1000 convertible. We flew the car over to Le Touquet from Southend, on one of the old Silver City planes whose noses opened wide so that cars could drive up a ramp into the fuselage – they were converted from wartime transport aircraft – and then we drove all the way, without a single hitch.

The only moments of drama came in Moscow, where Jeffrey's Intourist guide was a secret rebel who expressed his opposition to Communism by wearing a Star and Stripes T-shirt and deliberately taking the Minor the wrong way along one-way streets. When the little car crept into Red Square and parked in the shade of the Kremlin walls it drew a crowd almost as big as the queue for Lenin's tomb. The police, luckily, were as intrigued as everyone else.

> There'd never been a light blue Morris Minor 1000, number 3318UA, on those historic stones before. It was wonderful. It never let us down. I was so proud of it. I was particularly proud that it was British. You know, the Morris Minor 1000 was one of those archetypal British cars that a lot of people could afford. It had a choke, it had a starting handle, so that when it got cold, I could start it. When it had punctures, I could change the wheel. It never needed anything serious doing to it, so it was my car, and I could look after it. But I must admit that when I occasionally see them today, I think 'By Jove, did I drive all the way to Moscow in one of those little things?' And the answer is: 'Yes, I did.'

Shortly after this, I got a letter from Roger Wolstenholme who lives on a farm near Halifax and had heard what I was up to. He had also been behind the Iron Curtain, not long after Jeffrey, on a contract installing milking parlours in huge collective state farms in Poland and East Germany. He took his 1963 Rose Taupe Traveller, which he was properly proud of as a relatively new car. But that wasn't the attitude he met in the Communist countries. 'They all expected a Western car to be the latest thing and were absolutely astonished that I had one which seemed to be made of wood,' he said. He got plenty of opportunity to stop and pick up these comments, because the rutted roads in southern Poland took off the Traveller's exhaust four times – luckily the simplicity of the engineering meant that local workshops always fitted it smartly back on. But the delays gave time for the locals' fascination with the wooden framework of the Traveller to go further. Like Bridget Johnson's children with their fungus, people neatly removed splinters of the wood with penknives as souvenirs. 'I came back with these strange knife-marks all over the back,' said Wolstenholme. Alas, I couldn't count his chipped-at Traveller in my survey as it perished long ago, and Wolstenholme no longer runs a Minor. 'I would love to have a convertible,' he told me, 'but my wife won't have anything Morris Minor-related. She says they remind her of her aunt taking her to Sunday School.'

Is there something about Yorkshiremen, Morris Minors and an urge to see the world? I ask, because, just as the clock ticked down towards the end of my five-month survey, I struck gold again. I had arranged to have lunch with Tony Harcup, a lecturer in journalism at Sheffield University, who interviewed me for his book *The Ethical Journalist* and wanted a chat because he was updating it for a new edition. 'OK,' I said, 'but in return, is there anything you can tell me about Morris Minors?' 'No,' he said, 'but let's have lunch anyway.' I agreed, and I'm glad I did. When I arrived at Casa Mia in Chapel Allerton, an area nicknamed the Hampstead of Leeds, Tony passed me a grubby bit of paper with a scribble on it saying 'Joss Browning – by Morris Minor round the world.' After we'd finished, he said: 'Joss Browning now; if you've got five minutes, come and see this.'

We crossed Harrogate Road and walked down a side turning to a patch of rough ground on which stood one of the most exotic Morris Minors I have ever seen. Two petrol cans were bolted on a metal extension sticking out from the boot, which carried a spare wheel, with another bolted down on the roof. Twin spotlights were fixed to the top of the windscreen on either side and huge bull bars reached out beyond the front of the bonnet. Between them and the radiator was a business-like winch. The car was off-white but its colour had almost disappeared under a host of slogans about Round the World trips.

This was AHJ 567A, the heroic little car which took Joss Browning, a Leeds mechanic specialising in Morris Minors, through all six continents on a six-year journey starting in 1990. Feeling a bit limited by life in Leeds, Browning kitted out the 1957 four-door with a 1275cc MG Midget engine and a five-speed Toyota gearbox, using every available space for supplies, including spare room under the bonnet, where he stored firewood. Before leaving Yorkshire he also fitted and trialled a chicken-wire basket round the exhaust manifold which slow-cooked fish or meat and potatoes wrapped in foil as the car chugged along. Optimum cooking-while-driving time was two hours. Browning set off with an apprentice from his Major Minor Centre plus the lad's girlfriend, but when the latter's pregnancy became obvious and a bit of a risk issue in the wilds of Australia, he carried on alone. In Chile he met Lidia Defanchi and resumed the car's slow exploration of the world's roads. Most memorably, they parked at a ranch in Guatemala next to a long-abandoned mid-1950s Morris Minor 1000 and were surrounded in the middle of the night by a posse of armed men. Joss had been up late reading under his own Minor's rear spotlight, and once everything had been explained, the leader of the gang apologised.

We saw through the trees that the old car, abandoned eight years ago by a ranch hand who was fired for rustling, had come to life, with lights blazing. We thought that you were some kind of phantom.

Well, that was it, I thought. The publisher's deadline was approaching, and the world-conquering AHJ 576A was a high to go out on. Not counting the forty in Charlie Ware's workshop but including the Farndale rally, my tally was twenty Minors in five months. Admittedly, this didn't include the bulk of the summer, when the cars of weather-conscious owners are supposed to venture out, but it shows to my mind how rare the car is becoming. And yet it remains such an icon, whose reputation shows no sign of fading. I was pondering this and what to do next, when I hit the final jackpot. The White Rabbit appeared again.

I take my mother shopping most weeks, and the area in which I had spotted the Trafalgar Blue convertible lies between her home and ours. So, instead of going the quick way via the Leeds ring road, I took to threading my way through Adel, Ireland Wood and Cookridge, hoping to see the car once again. On 5 June it happened, at the other end of New Adel Lane. As I waited to turn right, up to Cookridge, the Minor suddenly appeared in front of me on Otley Old Road, turned into my road and trumpeted off. To the astonishment of one car behind me and another ahead, I did a police-style U-turn and followed. The Moggy had a start but I saw the fawn hood turn left just in time, and then we were in a maze of side roads lined with bungalows built by plot-holders in the 1920s behind the main Adel parade of shops. No Minor in view, and I reached a junction. I chose right, and curved round. Nothing to be seen. Then far ahead, just before it was blotted out of sight by a white removal van, I saw the fawn hood again. I caught up, just as the Minor stopped and dropped off a woman with short red hair and a big grin.

I nearly waylaid her, but decided to follow the car instead, catching up with it at traffic lights when it doubled back towards Leeds on Otley Road. It was sunny, the front windows were down and I asked the man with a neat beard at the wheel: 'Could I have a very quick word if you could pull up ahead?' 'I'm sorry,' he said, no doubt expecting some tedious Minor fan or an unwanted offer for the car. 'I'm meeting someone. I just haven't time.'

I couldn't pursue him after that, but equally I couldn't let the dark blue rabbit go. I drove back to the street where the woman passenger had got out. I couldn't remember the exact spot, but the removal van was mercifully still there. 'Did you see a woman get out of a Morris Minor a few minutes ago?' I asked the guys shifting furniture, feeling like a detective, albeit one on a mad errand. They looked me up and down, decided I was sane and said: 'She's inside.' She was, and amazingly, she looked at me and sad: 'Hello Martin.'

She was Dianne Riding, primary-school teacher extra-ordinaire to my two sons at Rawdon St Peter's infant and junior. That had been fifteen years earlier, but you don't forget a classroom festooned with everything brightly-coloured and imaginable, and she'd also had some A-level grade arguments with my highly logical and persistent older son Tom. I gaped and then explained, and out came a final, bull's-eye Morris Minor experience. 'It's mine,' she said. 'Duncan [the man with the beard] got it for me for my birthday a few years back.' At this point Duncan himself appeared and, once he had got over the fact that the wild man at the traffic lights was now in his new house, finished the story. 'I knew Dianne had learned to drive in a Morris Minor, and that she was after a car,' he said. He bought the convertible and then got a friend to paint a model the exact colour with the right number plate. Beautifully wrapped in a small box, this was handed on The Day to Dianne, who opened it – no doubt expecting jewellery, said Duncan – and looked at the model, saying something like: 'Oh, that's nice.' 'Then I told her: Now go and look outside,' said

Duncan. 'And that *was* nice.' We settled down to talk, and I told them about my mission, my adventures among Morris Minors and how I had decided early on that I needed to pay a visit to the source of them all. That is how it was that, a few months earlier, I had found myself on the City 5 bus bowling through the eastern suburbs of Oxford. Next stop: the site of Lord Nuffield's famous works in Cowley.

Chapter 3
Making History

Lord Nuffield hated the Morris Minor as soon as he saw it.
                                        Sir Alec Issigonis

In a phrase, the world's best baby car.
                        Stirling Moss, *Daily Express*, 1953

 IT IS THREE O'CLOCK ON A Tuesday afternoon, and bingo is well under way at the Lord Nuffield Club on William Morris Close at Cowley in Oxford. From the wall of the downstairs lounge bar the proceedings are watched silently by the lord himself, in a blown up black-and-white photograph next to the future King Edward VIII at the launch of the sporty Morris Eight two-seater. Along the corridor in the Body Shop, club members are pedalling and marching away on exercise machines, while upstairs the Mini Room crèche has a stack of toys ready for the next lot of children dropped off by mums and dads registered for the aerobics class. The toddlers will also be overseen by a photograph of a genial Nuffield, stuffing two old white-paper fivers into a wartime Red Cross collecting tin for a fund-raising photograph. 'Five weeks' wages at the time,'

says Eddy Griffiths, the club's Mr Fixit and maintenance man, who worked at Morris Motors himself for forty years.

Half a mile down Hollow Way and along Cowley Road, a desolate roundabout houses a two-storey-high stone pillar, the Nuffield Needle – the official local tribute to the great man and his factory, which employed 28,000 people in its heyday but was demolished in 1993. The needle's only decorations are two mischievous-looking oxen crossing fords on opposite sides of its base (the city's crest, and once the car company's); the sculptor definitely gave the ox looking back towards the dreaming spires a wink. All around are the modern offices of the Oxford Business Park, with notices warning that their pavements are not public property. Look hard, and you will find a small stone on one verge with a smaller plaque explaining that the needle was given by Arlington Securities, the park's developers.

That may be where most of the world's 1,600,000 Minors actually rolled off the production lines between 1948 and 1971 – but their best memorial is back at the Lord Nuffield Club, with Eddy and his former workmates playing bingo. When the number-calling breaks for tea, they take no persuading at all to return to the days of piecework, fitting clips to contels (the furry strips which wipe side-windows when you roll them down) and slicing seventy cow hides a shift to make leather for the base and back of four hundred Morris Minor seats.

That was Eddy's work for fifteen of his forty years, once he graduated to the cutting room, or trim shop, after a couple of years of the factory's dogsbody status of 'boy'. He joined at fifteen – 'on the twenty-seventh of August 1950,' he says, remembering exactly, like all his friends in the bingo session.

> Boys started off doing all sorts of little bits and pieces and got less wages, but they soon had us fitting the clips to the contels. It was five or six to every strip, and you'd to do sixty an hour to earn your proper money.

Everyone rapidly got used to this piecework system and generally liked it, in Eddy's experience. Extra effort earned more pay.

Could it also lead to shoddy workmanship? Difficult, say the bingo veterans, because there was an inspector at the end of every process, and if the work wasn't up to scratch, you would soon know about it. It was all very public too. On the line cutting vionide, the leather lookalike which clad the sides of Morris Minor seats, there were eighteen trimmers seated at twenty-five-metre benches, working on rolls of the material which stood five feet high. 'It was like clockwork, like choreography,' says Eddy, thinking back to those 1950s days when assembly lines, like pylons, were the subject of comedians' latest jokes. Much thinner than the leather, vionide was sliced fifty sheets at a time and taken over to the all-woman sewing shop for stitching together. The completed cover went on to the upholsterers – all men – who fitted it to seat frames, which were then trucked down to the actual car assembly line. Seats and cars came together in a precise sequence, the colour of the seat trim matching the colour of the car. 'Like choreography,' says Eddy again, admiringly. 'We had all differently shaped wooden patterns for when we were cutting the leather, and you had to get on with it. You needed to do ten hides an hour to earn your money.'

The system had the fascination of all mass-production work, and Nuffield himself (and, on one occasion Eddy recalls, Alec Issigonis) came to watch it in full swing. For their part, the cutters were taken to London to be lectured about the leather by its suppliers, the specialist firm Connolly's. The hides arrived at Cowley with felt fitted to one side and painted in Morris Minor interior colours on the other, but they were still cow-shaped. Warming to his memories, Eddy borrows my pen and draws one, a pancake-flat, headless oval seen from above, with two rectangles sticking out on either side which were once the hide round the animal's legs. 'That was the best bit,' he says, drawing two dotted lines the length of the oval, which would have run along the cow's flanks. 'The belly leather was too soft to be of any use. We cut that out for things like the pull straps you used to have on Morris Minor doors.'

Then there were the scars from barbed wire. The trimmers hid them as best they could, but most bottoms and squabs (backs) of Minor seats will have a trace of one. The only leather without them came from cattle from Sweden, where barbed wire wasn't used, but these were reserved for commission jobs for Van Den Plas cars, a limited-edition marque otherwise assembled in London. Eddy remembers that it took up to seven hours at Cowley to build just one Van Den Plas seat.

The Griffiths surname points to Welsh stock, and Eddy's family were part of a Welsh diaspora that came to Oxford when Morris Motors mushroomed in the 1920s. Times were hard in South Wales, and news spread that not that far down the A40 a Mr Morris (another Welsh name, although Nuffield's ancestors were actually Oxfordshire farmers) was making every other car produced in Britain. Some people even walked, according to Arthur Davis – another Minor veteran who worked in Cowley's tuning department, looking at electrical and mechanical rejects and trying to put them right. A kindly man with a fine head of hair at 78, he started at the works on 13 December 1954 and spent time on all the main assembly lines – including Wolseleys and Rileys as well as Morrises. But the Minor was his favourite, and, like Eddy and the others, he owned one, bought second-hand in 1955. 'They were so easy to work on, at home as well as in the factory. Most of the things that went wrong with them you could sort out in any reasonably-equipped garage.' He was interested in the car's development by Issigonis and remembers the change from side-valve to overhead engine and the loss of the split windscreen not long after he joined.

> We never saw Issigonis, mind you. Our workshop wasn't in his part of the manor. Lord Nuffield was often about though, wandering round C Block. He liked to be part of things.

Compared to other models, the Minor made relatively few appearances in Arthur's tuning 'hospital', so he remembers the main weaknesses which brought them back.

> Resetting the suspension was one of them. There was a regular fault in the torsion bar, and another bugbear was the lower swivel. The thread used to wear out.'

Firing up, but risking losing me in the technical details, he added: 'The wing piping at the rear gave us a lot of trouble. That was always needing welding.'

With the tea break still in full swing, Joan Vizer came and joined us with her cuppa and biscuit. She did thirty-five years at Cowley – not sewing Eddy's leather and vionide but in the publishing and printing department. She helped with both the technical Minor handbooks and all the cheerful advertisements and brochures which began the car's legend as the very stuff of Olde England. 'You name it, we published it,' she says. 'Puffs for the Motor Show and foreign exhibitions as well.' Pushing out all the material persuaded her to buy a Morris Minor herself in 1956 when she was twenty-seven.

> It was a green saloon. Oh, I loved my little Minor. I got a bit fed up with the way the door sills rusted, but I'd have kept it, only my son wanted a car to learn with, and Minors were ideal for that. So I passed it on.

News of what I was up to had meanwhile spread, and the

next table joined in, while the bingo callers patiently waited for the Minor mania to calm down. Alan Patterson and Bill Johns – another of the Cowley Welsh – went into instant nostalgia mode about the model's assembly line.

Oh it was well built, especially for a car at that time. All the metalwork was a lot thicker than what we use on these boxy cars today. And it was a fun place, too. Everyone was more or less happy, weren't they, Bill?

Bill Johns agreed, although he recalled very little time for anything other than work, between the permitted rest and meal breaks. The lines ran on the remorseless tracking method invented by Henry Ford, and the pace of work couldn't slow without risking everything coming to a halt. Bill was appointed in 1954 as the first 'relief man' on the Morris Minor line. Until he arrived, if one of the team was ill or needed a lavatory break, or just slowed down, the rest could only cover by taking up the slack between them.

The piecework rates kept us happy, and we all took a pride in the job. You could work rapidly because you knew your job thoroughly. Every man was an expert.

Lord Nuffield and the likes of Issigonis were at the top of this tree but they also got respect because they so obviously knew what they were doing too. Nuffield's philanthropy accounts for part of his lasting reputation – he is not seen by any of the bingo veterans as an exploitative, us-and-them, boss. They list not only his famous good works, in the obvious shape of hospitals and Oxford University's Nuffield College (with its motto *Fiat lux*, which may or may not have been a donnish prank), but also less well-known ones. 'He gave this here club to the workforce,' says Eddy Griffiths. 'They set up a committee, and he gave it to them and said: "You get on with it." ' After a troubled period recently, the present management has done his financial memory proud. They sold the original Morris Sports and Social Club building down the road to developers at a profit which paid for the smart – and much bigger – new Lord Nuffield Club, which opened just before Christmas 2007.

'It's just a shame he didn't have sons,' says Eddy, who remembers management passing to outsiders from Austin – the ancient, deadly rival to Morris – with the merger into the British Motor Corporation in 1952. Things got progressively more grim. Gradually piecework was replaced with 'measured daywork': standard shifts which reduced the direct connection between pay and productivity. Research and design slipped too. There was the glorious reign of the Mini, strictly speaking the Morris Mini-Minor, Issigonis's second and most famous creation, which appeared in 1959 and accounted for a British record of 5.3 million cars made over forty-one years. But, that aside, the name of Morris became associated with a range of unmemorable models, such as the Marina, Maestro, and Metro and, alphabetically distinguished if in no other way, the Ital.

*

Those were very different from the car that went through the hands of Eddy, Arthur, Alan, Joan and Bill. The Minor had its origins in a famous runabout that was the Mini of its day when it was launched in 1922, the Austin Seven. Designed to be no bigger than the billiard table at Herbert, later Lord, Austin's home, Lickey Grange near Birmingham, this was the first real attempt at a 'people's car' in Britain. It wiped out competitors and became famous in anecdote and even ballad, usually on account of its small size relative to cumbersome and expensive predecessors. My parents taught us as children the limerick:

> The Bishop has got a new Austin.
> He finds it very exhaustin'.
> His head and his knees
> Get in with a squeeze,
> But the rest of him has to be forced in.

Because we pronounced Austin to rhyme with 'lost in', the curious half-rhymes have found a permanent place in the lumber room of my mind.

It was an Austin Seven that Alec Issigonis bought as his first car when he left Battersea College in 1928, after failing his maths exams three times but excelling at drawing. He had got a job in a small London engineering company and needed wheels. He was helped by his mother, who sold a diamond ring to raise the balance of the £160-odd purchase price (£6,600 today). Issigonis had previously messed around in, and with, a Blériot Whippet, one of the three-wheeled cyclo-cars which were the first step to motoring at the time for enthusiasts with limited funds. He was fascinated by the advanced mechanical design of the Austin, its excellent suspension and lightweight engine, which was easy to dismantle and maintain. Later, in his spare time from Morris Motors (whom he joined in 1935 as a Design Department suspension and steering engineer, after a couple of years working on Humbers with the Rootes empire), he cannibalised parts from an Austin Seven Sports to build a graceful, fast and innovative racing car by hand.

He called it the Lightweight Special, and its novelties, such as independent rubber suspension at both front and rear and a body and chassis moulded as a single piece of plywood faced with aluminium – like aircraft of the period – have attracted much interest. Modern admirers are naturally curious, partly because of Issigonis's later achievements; however, contemporaries at the time who saw the car realised that its young designer was brimming with fresh but practical ideas.

The Special first raced in 1938, but within a year Issigonis's creativity with civilian cars was put on hold. The outbreak of war brought an end to new car production, and companies such as Morris were diverted full-time to military orders. Issigonis designed a two-man tank called the Nuffield Salamander and a giant amphibious wheelbarrow with balloon tyres and an outboard motor, the Nuffield Guppy, which was designed to enable troops to carry war supplies dropped by parachute. His skill with suspension and light engines was evident in both, but neither went further than the prototype. The war, however, led to an encounter crucial to the process that created the Morris Minor.

Fire-watching at the huge and vulnerable Cowley plant was a vital duty during the blitz. It introduced a rough industrial democracy, where shop-floor workers could find themselves on overnight duty with members of senior management. One night in 1940 Issigonis found himself looking out for incendiaries with the company's Chief Engineer, Vic Oak, and its Vice-Chairman, Miles Thomas, who was second only to Lord Nuffield. Thomas was a genial former journalist who shared Issigonis's enthusiasm for motor racing. Trained as a pilot in the Royal Flying Corps, he had covered major European race meetings in the early 1920s by plane, looping above the circuits and filing his reports to newspapers and magazines immediately on landing. Unusually for a journalist, he was also a very good manager. Hired initially by Nuffield to pioneer PR, which he did with élan, he transferred to head the Wolseley division before becoming Nuffield's deputy in 1940. In his memoirs *Out on a Wing*, he vividly remembered this first encounter with Issigonis, and the conviction it gave him that the young designer was a man with fundamental new ideas about cars.

Thomas had a hush-hush initiative which needed such a man. Because of the wartime ban on new cars, it had to be small and discreet, and it was given the military-sounding name of the Mosquito Project, after the lightweight RAF fighter bomber which Thomas the ex-pilot much admired.

He enlisted Issigonis to be its principal designer, helped by the less spectacular but sturdy and practical talents of Reg Job and William 'Jack' Daniels, under the experienced supervision of Vic Oak. For Issigonis, it was a dream come true after years of fiddling with detail on other designers' cars or toiling at unrewarding wartime projects.

It was from this point that he became known as the man at Cowley who lived and breathed motor car design to the exclusion of almost everything else. Thirty years later another of his colleagues in the late 1940s, Eric Lord, recalled that Issigonis 'wasn't able to have a conversation without a pencil in his hand. The number of linen table cloths he ruined was legion.' When he ran out of paper, he chalked his ideas on the factory floor or drew them on discarded packets of the cigarettes he constantly smoked. He could never draw people (in all his surviving sketches, there is only one attempt to do so, and it is feeble) but his desk – and wastepaper basket – snowed up with paper covered in neat diagrams, equations and measurements. Through these gradually emerged the two great assets of the car that was to become the Morris Minor.

The first was rack-and-pinion steering, a revolution in British car design, which is portrayed in an Issigonis diagram on page 2 of Section J of the original Morris Minor Workshop Manual. Sixty-eight separate parts allowed a finely-machined metal wheel (the pinion) to engage with similar teeth on a two-foot horizontal bar (the rack) and thus to convert the rotating motion of the steering wheel to the linear motion of the front wheels. It gave the driver an unprecedented feeling of control with a smoothness that anticipated the much later invention of power steering and the all-but-universal adoption of rack-and-pinion systems in modern cars. The principle was certainly not Issigonis's invention: John Blenkinsop had used it on the Middleton colliery railway in 1811, and a handful of early and expensive cars had tried it for steering. But in cheap and mass-production cars, which had previously stuck to worm-and-peg gearing systems to steer, it was novel indeed.

The second outstanding piece of mechanics was the suspension, Issigonis's long-standing speciality, which also has a lovely diagram of its own in Section K of the manual. A total of eighty-eight parts figure here for the front suspension alone, which used torsion bars to give each wheel independent suspension. The result was superbly improved road-holding. Separate, independent rear suspension was part of Issigonis's original design, but was vetoed reluctantly by Miles Thomas as too expensive for a £100 car. The traditional leaf spring system was adopted instead: less efficient but using the delicate curves of metal strips which are familiar to all Minor users who have changed a flat tyre.

The wheels we lugged off the hub-bolts after a puncture were another innovation, the smallest yet fitted to a mass-production British car. Fourteen inches in diameter, compared to seventeen on standard models such as the Morris Eight, they were positioned right at the corners of the chassis, imparting extra grip to the road-holding and adding extra room to the passenger compartment. This was a final, radical innovation and a Holy Grail for Issigonis throughout his working life. Anticipating the miracle he was later to work with the apparently tiny but actually very spacious Mini, he pushed the Minor's engine as far forward as he dared, which gave significant extra comfort and leg-stretching space inside.

With a portfolio of radical new ideas like this, the Mosquito was certain to spring a dramatic surprise on the British car market, and the effect was completed by its streamlined bodywork. The curves that over the years have earned the Morris Minor a name for cosy British homeliness were actually an American import, and pretty hot stuff; at the time they were the 'latest thing', along with chewing gum, milk shakes and the bikini. Known as the 'New Look' (like Christian Dior's influential 1947 fashion collection), the bulbous humps, flush-fitted door handles and what Morris publicists were to refer to as 'air-flow body lines' came straight across the Atlantic from 'Chicago gangster' cars like the Oldsmobile and Cadillac. Other design references ranged from the curving, sculpted fridges newly-fashionable in New York to the huge, streamlined diesel locomotives that had replaced traditional smokestacks on America's railroads. The running boards and game-looking bolted-on spare wheels which had been such an essential part of previous, angular British car design were enclosed within the bodywork, giving yet more room inside.

The dramatic new small car was ready for a test run in the early summer of 1946, when a full-scale mahogany model of the Mosquito was prepared for Lord Nuffield, while Vic Oak took the prototype out for a spin and told Thomas that it was 'by far the best prototype car that I have ever been associated with.' However, larger events now came to bear on the project, first effectively freezing it, to the horror of all involved, then leading to the final changes that turned the Mosquito into the Minor.

Nuffield came, saw and made his famous comment to the design team ('It looks like a poached egg. We can't make that') – and it was apt, for if Oak and Issigonis had painted the prototype Mosquito's roof pale yellow and the rest of its bodywork white, a poached egg on wheels is what they would have had. Although theoretically an arm's-length chairman, and by this stage of his career undoubtedly more interested in philanthropy than innovatory car design, the Viscount had the power of veto. He blocked proposals to put the car into production and insisted instead on increasing the company's output of the Morris Eight, which as long ago as 1935 had taken over as the firm's main small car from the original 1928 Morris Minor. As Nuffield repeatedly told Thomas during prolonged arguments in late 1946 and throughout most of 1947, it was still in such demand that the firm had more orders than it could meet.

This was true but misleading. *All* cars were in enormous demand after the end of the war, once it suddenly became possible to buy new ones again. At the same time, the new Labour Government began an 'Export or Die' campaign to restore the country's ruined balance of payments and called on the motor trade to lead it. It is hard to imagine such centralised control and austerity today, but Morris, Austin and the other manufacturers were required to sell three-quarters of their restarted civilian car production overseas, while the domestic market was rationed. Buyers had to put their names down months in advance and sign a promise not to sell on for at least a year, to deter profiteering. For a couple of years, disastrously, the car-makers could sell virtually anything to anyone – not just at home but in the precious export market, to other countries which had suffered worse devastation in the war and were only beginning to rebuild and retool their own motor plants. Production shot up from 17,000 cars nationally in 1945 to more than 216,000 the following year but with no new models joining the existing pre-war range. There was wild talk of selling twenty million cars to the Soviet Union alone, and in Lord Nuffield's mind these would all have been Morris Eights. The prevailing attitude was epitomised by Wolseley, a Morris subsidiary, which received complaints about a model whose gear stick regularly snapped at the base. Complainants were sent letters effectively advising them to learn how to change gear more carefully.

Petrol rationing, meanwhile, allowed only a hundred and fifty miles of motoring a month immediately after the war, falling to just eighty as the United States called in its war loans and austerity tightened its grip. British roads were meandering lanes, and there was no thought in transport planners' minds of copying Hitler's autobahns or Mussolini's autostradas. Cars were subject to the punitive twenty-five-year-old Horsepower Tax, which was based on engine size and so further deterred innovation. The tax had served the domestic manufacturers well in the earliest days of mass motoring by penalising the American invader, the Model T Ford (22.5hp, taxed at £23 – £650 today) compared to the Morris Cowley (11.9hp, paying £12 – £340 today). But now it was blocking Britain's own design progress. New thinking faced obstacles in every direction, quite apart from Nuffield's opposition.

Battle was joined on all fronts, with Thomas and Issigonis in the van. They knew that if their ideas were deep-frozen, rivals overseas would catch up, among them (as indeed happened) a Volkswagen business resurrected by British management, free of much Government bureaucracy and well aware of the asset it had in the Beetle. Both men pitched energetically into lobbying for tax reform, using their particular skills to intrigue the Labour Chancellor of the Exchequer, Hugh Dalton. He agreed to meet them and to make room at the Treasury for working wooden models which they took with them from Oxford of both a new and efficient engine of the type they wanted to use in the Mosquito, and a costly, ungainly one favoured by the Horsepower Tax. A distant relative of the Manchester scientist John Dalton, the Chancellor took the engineering points as well as the fiscal ones, to Thomas's eternal relief. 'He characteristically rolled his eyes upward,' Thomas said after the demonstration, 'and boomed: "I see you have a good case."'

Nuffield was a tougher prospect. His opposition to an entirely new car had some logic in short-term commercial thinking, but his temperament was also mercurial. He had made his millions and was increasingly more interested in giving them away than in using his once eager delight in new ideas to support changes at the car factory. He had always been nervy; colleagues were used to his constant worries about illness, leading to remedies such as glasses of bicarbonate of soda before important meetings that were then punctuated by burps and worse. Like his great rival Lord Austin, he had developed a fierce fondness for his past achievements. Both magnates had a particular thing about radiators, and Nuffield could not bear the thought of losing the vertical, centre-split Morris shape with its proud ox-and-ford badge, which he had made his own. He also greatly disliked the name Mosquito – so exotically and poisonously different from his previous, homely choices – and was instrumental in the change to Morris Minor at the very end of 1947. It was not his idea, but one of many ploys by the car's supporters to win him over and end what the exasperated Thomas called his 'sulky lack of enthusiasm' and persistence in 'exercising his right of destructive criticism.' Many years later in *Out on a Wing*, Thomas revealed that at the height of this dismal and soul-destroying struggle, he was offered more money and every freedom in an invitation from Austin to join them as joint chief executive with Len Lord, later Lord Lambury (another outstanding manager driven from Cowley in the mid-1930s by similar frustration with Nuffield). Out of loyalty, and providentially for the Morris Minor, Thomas refused to follow Lord's example.

It was only a matter of time, though, and finally he did leave the company – in November 1947 after twenty-three years' service – to a series of grudging mumbles from

Nuffield and a £10,000 honorarium (£270,000 today). He did not go to Austin but into temporary retirement, before changing tack completely and becoming chairman of the new British Overseas Airways Corporation. The crucial fact was that he had won the Morris Minor battle at last and wanted a rest and, once the new car's future was absolutely secure, an escape from Nuffield. On 10 November 1947, just one day before his resignation as managing director was accepted, Thomas was at last able to sign an incontrovertible instruction for 50,000 models to go into production. They were to be ready to go on sale on New Year's Day 1949, with a dozen completed two months earlier for the 1948 Motor Show in London.

The car reluctantly approved by Nuffield incorporated significant deviations from Issigonis's original design, just as the ground-breaking independent rear suspension had been dropped for pricing reasons by Thomas. The most disappointing was the replacement of a new and powerful engine designed by Issigonis by a slightly enhanced version of the one used in Nuffield's beloved Morris Eight. This had long-term consequences, especially for exports to the United States, where a more powerful engine might have won the Minor the place eventually taken by the VW Beetle. But the other (and most extraordinary) change was Issigonis's own inspiration: he made a truly spectacular last-minute adjustment to the size and shape of the car.

Like all designers, Issigonis spent hour after hour observing things minutely and thinking about them, but the long gestation of the Mosquito had made him familiar with its every detail to the point of dullness. There come moments when the veil imposed by such immensely detailed, close-up study is suddenly lifted by standing back and emptying your mind: the solution to the old problem of failing to see the wood for the trees. Issigonis had a remarkable such moment one evening in late 1947 (the date has sadly never been pinned down).

Referring back to his many drawings, and then the prototype in its workshop at Cowley, he instructed his startled mechanics to split the body in half from bonnet to boot. The following morning, the two half-cars were raised on blocks and moved to and fro, pausing at distances measured in fractions of an inch, until Issigonis signalled a halt. The gap stood at four inches, and it removed the subconscious nag in his mind that the new car's shape had not been quite right. Thanks to the skill of Reg Job, who added metal strips to the floor, roof and bonnet, a wider version of the prototype was created without any need for changes to the engine, transmission and other mechanical parts. The only evidence was a four-inch metal fillet in the middle of the front and rear bumpers which became (and remains) a distinction of the earliest batch of the car, the Series MM manufactured between 1948 and 1953. Miles Thomas was delighted, the poached egg was noticeably less ovoid, and the car gained in roominess, stability and road-holding. The shape of the Morris Minor was finally set.

Progress was rapid, once Lord Nuffield had been squared, and the Minor was a triumph at the 1948 Motor

Show at Earl's Court in London, where attendance of over half a million people doubled any previous year's total. Post-war interest in motoring was reviving, and although new exhibits included the sleekly beautiful Jaguar XK10 sports car, the biggest crowds gathered around the Minor stand. The two Bibles of the motorist, *Autocar* and *Motor* magazines, were unanimous in praise. *Autocar* described the car as 'a triumph in good looks' as well as remarkably advanced mechanically for a small and economical model. *Motor* said simply that the Minor stole the show – this at the head of a review so thorough that it tested how comfortably the car treated a passenger who wanted to write a letter and then nod off to sleep during a journey. It was approved on both counts, and *Motor* added perceptively (in the light of the way successive generations have come to see the Morris Minor) that it had 'a charm of its own.'

The media was skilfully courted, of course, by Issigonis's PR colleagues, who used the story of his late-night splitting of the prototype to good effect. Press material described how the shifting of the two halves had continued until 'proportion was propitiated and harmony satisfied', and referred almost eugenically to the incident's creation of 'a new breeding line' for the company's future cars. Technically and on price, as well as in stylish design, the Minor also saw off the rivals in its class which other carmakers unveiled at Earl's Court. It was smaller and cheaper than Austin's A40 and A70 and the new Jowett Javelin from Bradford, while Ford's Anglia and Prefect seemed old-fashioned because they had stuck to pre-war, boxy looks.

Demand for the Minor was immediately enormous, and waiting lists placed Morris Motors under such pressure that in 1949 two new assembly lines were created at Cowley to increase output. Issigonis was given a walloping pay rise, from £960 before tax to £1,500 (£23,500 and £36,600 today) and enjoyed his first taste of being lionised as the exceptional designer he had long believed himself to be. The rest of his team were also fêted. Although in his later years, Sir Alec sometimes described proudly how he had designed even the smallest details, including the knob on the glove box, he acknowledged that Oak, Job and Daniels had been crucial to the project's success. Thomas, likewise, and other sources of inspiration also got deserved credit, especially a fellow-expert in suspension, Maurice Olley of Vauxhall, who shared Issigonis's complete absorption in the subject and had often discussed it with him before the war.

There was one predictable spectre at the feast. Lord Nuffield refused to go on any test drives or even to be photographed in the car at the Motor Show, in spite of the fact that ordinary punters had been cramming on to the back bench-seat four at a time. The Minor was like a child with a cold-hearted, uninterested and perhaps jealous father. If we were to anthropomorphise it in the manner of Beatrix Potter with her rabbits, its extraordinary success could be ascribed to a determination to prove its parent wrong, like so many famous lonely children, from Sir Winston Churchill to Frank Sinatra. Buyers who got an early Morris, gave it a pet name and read of Nuffield's well-publicised snub would certainly have felt like that, and in their small way helped to make the analogy real. As we shall see, the Viscount was going to face further embarrassing public celebrations of the poached egg and would eventually swallow his pride.

For the time being, however, the success of the Minor and its associated new models, including the Morris Oxford Series MO, the Morris Six Series M6 and two Wolseleys, ushered in a new era at Cowley. Within four years Issigonis had left for Alvis; Morris and Austin had merged; and Nuffield had finally withdrawn from active involvement – in 1952, at the age of 75, retiring to the honorary position of President of the new joint company, the British Motor Corporation. The Minor itself marched on. And so did I, back on to the bus – whose advertisements for inventive new carbon-reducing engines might have interested Issigonis – and then on the train to Angmering in West Sussex.

Chapter 4
The Morris Million

Der Morris Minor hat viele Freunde auf der ganzen Welt.
Auto Exclusiv magazine, Germany, 1987

IT IS A FAMILIAR SIGHT: a Morris Minor with its big domed bonnet open and its owner bent underneath to tinker with something in the engine compartment. This one is parked in the sunshine on the gravel drive of Richard Elderfield's stockbroker-Tudor house next to Angmering golf course. However, it is in no way ordinary. For one thing, it is the most peculiar colour. Purple vomit, some people have called it; 'the colour of sick,' says Charlie Ware more prosaically. 'Mister, why did you get your car painted that revolting colour?' teenagers call to Andrew Dyer, managing director in the south of England for the Stagecoach travel company, when he goes for a run in his Minor, which is painted the same odd shade.

These remarks are about the Morris Million, the rarest of all the Minor sub-species. Only 349 were made in the first place, and today we know the whereabouts of just sixty-three of them. One is more significant than all the others, though: the one on Richard Elderfield's drive, with its battery hopelessly flat. Look beneath the conveniently open bonnet, and a manufacturer's metal tag on the left, above the engine, says 'Cowley M/A2S3 1000000'. The bonnet might be a bit wonky – 'It sometimes flies open when we're out for a drive,' says Richard's son Neil, as he tries in vain to find a spark of electrical life – but this was the millionth Morris Minor to be made.

It was also the first British car to take a marque past the million figure. That's not uncommon nowadays – the Mini sold 5,300,000 between 1958 and 2000 – but it was remarkable in 1960, when it made national headlines. Richard's car rolled off Assembly Line 1 at Cowley on 22 December, followed by a van and a Traveller estate. The British Motor Corporation, in its eighth year of producing Minors after taking over from Morris Motors, made a great hullabaloo of the occasion, and its public relations team thought of all sorts of extras. They published a commemorative booklet, *A Million Morris Minors*, which claimed (a little boldly) that a 1960 Morris Minor was cheaper than a 1948 one, allowing for adjustments in the value of the pound. Easier to substantiate, if laborious to peruse, were the book's production statistics. They included this : 'If all the Morris Minors which have left the production line at Cowley were spaced at intervals of 407 yards and 11½ inches, the first would rest in Oxfordshire and the millionth would have its wheels on the moon.' The PR people also lined seven Millions up in front of Blenheim Palace in a link with the aristocracy which was to continue. When the earliest Morris to be made was tracked down many years later the Duke of Bedford was persuaded to be photo-graphed outside Woburn Abbey sitting in it and, for some reason, having a shave. Another deliberate eye-catcher was the millionth Minor's distinctive numberplate, 1 MHU (Mhu is one spelling of classical Greek's abbreviation of a million).

It was the numberplate which attracted Richard's interest thirty years ago when – as I discovered to my delight when we met beside his lifeless car – he was in charge of all the country's Cadbury's chocolate vending machines. As a young reporter on the London *Evening Standard* and later the *Guardian*, I used to get lunch from these – and, if I was constantly on the hop, breakfast and tea as well. There was one in every London Tube station in the early 1970s, and a Cadbury's fruit-and-nut bar had all the sustenance I needed. 'So I helped pay for this car,' I suggested. In fact, though, no money had changed hands. Richard came across his unique piece of history when it was in a very sorry state.

'Neil was really responsible,' he says. Now forty-three and a builder and landscape gardener on the East Sussex coast, Elderfield junior used to love riding round in the back of a Morris Minor pickup at the farm in Wales where the family stayed when he was a small boy. This was at Penrhiwillan, near Newcastle Emlyn in Cardiganshire, and the Elderfields knew most of the locals, including the postman Ivor Jones. Noting Neil's enthusiasm for the Minor, Jones told him, when the family where staying there in 1972: 'I've got one those but she's not in very good nick.' He had rolled her over on one of the narrow roads and ended up in a ditch; the roof had a deep furrow in it and the front wing on the driver's side had crumpled and come off. 'I'll show her to you,' said Jones, and off they all trooped to a nearby barn.

Here on chocks stood a red Morris Minor. I would have said bright red, but Elderfield's photographs taken at the time show the bodywork coated with a yellowy grime. She looks a most unappealing car, even to a Minor enthusiast; a Post Office van gone wrong – but one with this highly desirable registration. Richard had enough spare money to indulge himself, and in buying the numberplate he agreed to take the car as well. He could slowly restore it as a long-term project for when the highly delighted Neil was older. Another photograph shows the new owners beaming beside a rescue truck which took the Minor back to their home in Warwickshire and a temporary nest in a chicken shed. In a handy bit of bartering, Jones parted with the car in return for Richard installing central heating in his cottage, a job he eventually contracted-out to a local plumber because of the demands of managing chocolate vending machines.

Jones had told Elderfield that the car had some sort of special pedigree, but not one in which he had taken any great interest. It was almost certainly a Morris Million, because it had 1,000,000 instead of 1000 in small chrome numbers on the boot and wings. But, apart from such minor details, Millions were basically the same as any other Minor, and 1972 was perhaps the nadir of the make's fortunes. Production had only stopped the previous year, and the car was not yet old enough to be a classic. It was for aunts and students and people learning to drive. The Mini was the cool equivalent, basking in the lustre of the 1969 Michael Caine comedy film *The Italian Job*.

Elderfield was intrigued, however, and then, like me at Angmering, he looked under the bonnet and saw the 1,000,000 registration tag. It clicked. Could this possibly be *the* millionth, the Million of Millions? He checked out the log book and found more significant evidence. The car had never strayed very far in the eighteen years before Ivor rolled it into the ditch. Originally registered at a garage in Bristol, so that it could qualify for the regional HU in its numberplate, its first owner had been a Susan George of Llechrydd, a pretty village just outside Cardigan where Penny and I once had an idyllic holiday when our oldest son Tom was one. And, look at this: in the log book column for colour was written the word 'Lilac', scored through and replaced by 'Red'.

Definitely a genuine Million, then, because no other car used Purple Vomit; and further research soon established 1 MHU's glorious pedigree. The millionth car had indeed gone to a Miss George of Llechrydd, although not Susan. It was the prize in a national raffle which was part of BMC's promotional razzamatazz (the firm cunningly gave the car to the National Union of Journalists to raise money for the Red Cross) and the winner was Mrs George's daughter. She was too young to drive but she knew which colours she liked – and didn't. Of all the Millions, the millionth had its curious livery for the shortest time.

Does it matter which car or homeowner or tourist

actually represents the magic number when a product or tally of anything passes a landmark? We seem to think so. One of my cousins was surprised on a visit to Sri Lanka five years ago to be greeted at Colombo airport by flashing camera bulbs, attractive young women and a garland of fresh flowers. He thought he had been mistaken for one of the current Hollywood hunks, but it turned out, more prosaically, that he was the country's five-hundred-thousandth visitor that year. Luckily, his companion, who was also garlanded, was someone he was entitled to be with, and everyone was very pleased.

There is often a catch, though, in these ceremonies, just as on several occasions recently television voting has been shown to be a travesty of what really went on. Was my cousin really the half-millionth visitor, or had he fitted conveniently into staff shifts at the airport and the local media's preferred deadlines? Equally, was 1 MHU the car which received all the publicity in 1960 as the millionth Minor, or was it the victim of early spin? We will probably never know, but the Morris Million Owners' Club has sown the seeds of doubt, through the sort of relentless, focused research which marks all such excellent enthusiasts. The caption to the official photograph taken by BMC shows the car coming off the assembly line as described on 22 December 1960. But . . . what is this? . . . the photo itself was taken on 12 December, ten days earlier.

A misprint? Another car used, so that the publicity material could be guaranteed ready for immediate release after the actual event on 22 December, when Issigonis and a colleague called L. Bowles could be present? It is a mystery better left unfathomed. Those in charge at BMC are no longer with us, and the Red Cross told me, with regret, that they had no record of the raffle in their archives. My own trade union, the National Union of Journalists, chosen to receive the car by BMC's canny press office, had also forgotten, although its deputy general secretary John Frey was interested in knowing more. He had worked at Cowley himself for a time, and his father-in-law was a mechanic at the plant with a name as the fastest tyre fitter on the Morris Minor line. John told me:

> People used to ask him: 'How do you do it, Wally? What's the secret?' because he was an artful bloke, brought up in a boys' home. It was all in the soap. He'd say: 'Get yourself a bar of soap and whip it round the rim. The tyre'll go on as easy as winking.' And it did.

There had been enormous changes at Cowley after the Austin–Morris merger into BMC, but the Minor had continued to prosper through it all. The industry was developing its reputation for dismal labour relations, foreign competition was growing, and the Mini stole much of the Minor's glory and all Alec Issigonis's interest when the great designer returned from three years in exile at Alvis, where his stylish and powerful new saloon was scrapped at the last moment as too expensive. Fortunately, he had laid such substantial groundwork that the Minor developed successfully in other hands. Jack Daniels had taken over when Issigonis left in 1952, and he was almost as familiar with the car. He was also able to build on initial plans for improving the car which Issigonis had begun to sketch out. A four-door saloon had already appeared, in 1950, and the first of the timber-framed Travellers, which were to become an icon within an iconic marque, were produced in 1953.

The shape of the Minor had also settled down, with the scrapping of the 'low light' original, much to the sadness of Issigonis. He was particularly pleased with the look of the first two years' production of the MM series whose headlights were placed low down below the bonnet on either side of the 'smiling' radiator grille, in accordance with the best American streamlining principles. But it was an American decision which forced their removal. 'Export or Die' remained the Labour Government's watchword, and in 1949 Californian headlamp legislation made lights as low-slung and centralised as the Minor's illegal. The ban was followed by other states and was widely expected to spread to Europe, so the lights were moved to their now familiar position at the front of the car's wings, not just in US export models but for the entire run. The change reduced the car's top speed by an estimated 1.5 mph, giving Issigonis the satisfaction of seeing his airflow principles borne out, but it also settled the Minor look that has been familiar for so long. It is the 'low lights', actually the original design, which now appear an oddity.

The split-screen front window, one of the results of Issigonis's famous bisection of the Mosquito prototype, went next. It was dropped in 1956 as part of a radical update which introduced the most lasting and popular of the car's models, the Minor 1000. The one-piece windscreen was not just a cosmetic, modernising change in the Minor's outside appearance but had real benefits for drivers: the split screen had been prone to leak and was not entirely covered by the primitive wipers. The standard-issue Series MM had only one wiper, a second one for the passenger side being available only as an optional extra. The original workshop manual is an enlightening guide to similar crude aspects of the car, some of which survived until its final production months in 1971. For instance, it recommended tackling water penetration in the doors and wings with two proprietary glues, one of them Bostik, which was familiar to all amateur model-makers. Maybe this was part of the Minor's special charm, described by *Motor* on its 1948 debut, although the workshop manual was intended for garages rather than owners.

The important development in the Minor 1000 was under the bonnet, where it was fitted with a much more powerful engine: the A Series, which had overhead valves as originally intended by Issigonis. Power rose to 948cc and then 1098cc, giving the new model a name for nippiness, which BMC advertising reflected. This very nicely com- plemented the make's established reputation for sturdiness and reliability, which prompted *Motor* to welcome the Minor 1000 by saying 'There has never been a bad Morris Minor.' The show-jumper Pat Moss had just joined the BMC rallying team and was poised for the glories described

in Chapter 9, which showed both speed and extreme tough-
ness in her celebrated Minor nicknamed 'Granny'. Her
brother Stirling, the racing driver who was later knighted,
meanwhile tanked up his Minor with its distinctive MMM
numberplate and gave it fifteen per cent more power.

Moss was a favourite at the newsreel cinemas and on
television, and BMC did its best to make the Morris Minor
a film star as well. Promotional films initially focused on
reliability, as in *Dusty Road*, in which a saloon and a
convertible cross large parts of Canada in clouds of dust
from a gravel highway; it lasts 70 minutes and requires some
durability from its audience, unless they are particularly
interested in Canadian scenery. But the commentary leaves
no doubt about the sturdiness of the Minor and occasionally
bursts into passion, perhaps remembering the American
audience for which it was also designed: 'With foot hard
down' (a clip of yet another stretch of winding trail through
mountains and forests begins) 'and the thrill of sixty miles
an hour . . .'

A similar film, in 1952, condensed the action into half-
an-hour and chose the rather more interesting setting of
German autobahns near Stuttgart, where there were at least
people and other cars to be seen. Along with a Morris
Oxford and several Austins, a Minor was driven for 20,000
miles without mechanical faults of any kind. The convoy, all
painted black and looking from aerial shots like purposeful
beetles on a high-speed mission, keep overtaking the other
sort of Beetle. The commentary never says it, but the
message about VWs is clear, and I am sure newsreel cinema

audiences would have cheered. A third 'reliability' film from the company emphasises duration and setting even more, showing a Minor carrying out a 10,000-mile non-stop drive at Brooklands racing circuit. This is managed with the help of a BMC-designed tender with a rear section shaped like a tuning fork; for refuelling or changing drivers, the Minor nuzzles up between the fork's tines and is held there – while still using its own power. Men with clipboards and wall charts abound, and the whole effect is most impressive.

The Minor 1000's debut advertising continued the basic theme of a car which would not let you down, but added new emphasis on power and style. A chic young thing pilots a bright blue Minor nippily round London (where the lack of traffic in 1956 brings tears to modern eyes). As she parks to take photographs across the Thames from the South Bank, the commentary draws parallels between the car and sleek new Waterloo bridge, both masterpieces of engineering. The message is: Minor 1000, elegance, power and style. Brochures and advertisements in newspapers and magazines took the same line, with slogans such as 'Zip goes the 1000' and 'Now you move up *twice as fast* in the mighty Morris Minor.' (Nought to sixty in twenty-eight seconds, eh? Strewth!) References abound to whip-quick acceleration, power-boosts for a brisk-stepper and, significantly, the pleasures of 'big-car', long distance motoring. By the time these puffs appeared in 1957, work was starting on Britain's first motorways: the Ross Spur (off what is now the M5) and the London end of the M1.

The launch was timely in much wider social terms. At a speech in Bedford on 20 July, the Conservative Prime Minister Harold Macmillan made his famous observation that people in Britain had 'never had it so good'. The phrase became a hostage to fortune, as there were plenty of places that post-war economic revival had yet to reach, but his argument that the country as a whole was much more prosperous than at any time in his life – and indeed in its history – was undeniable. Average weekly earnings for men very nearly doubled in the 1950s, and by the time the Minor 1000 appeared, the professional middle classes were developing the habit of owning a second car. Advertisements from BMC played on this by showing a woman at the wheel and highlighting the amount of room for children and shopping. The fruits of self-denial and hard work during the austerity period seemed at last to be within reach. Although prices in general were rising, in relation to earning power the economies of mass production were leading to an actual fall in the cost of much new technology. Let's buy a television, a washing machine – and, even if we have to pay by instalments or on hire purchase (universally known at the time as 'the HP'), a Morris Minor 1000.

Look at the sales figures. In 1956 BMC sold 70,000 Minors; in 1957 104,000, and the figure stayed above 100,000 for the next two years. Not surprisingly, 1958 saw an historic tipping point in the history of transport in Britain: for the first time, more journeys were made in private cars than on buses and trains combined, a trend which has continued ever since.

*

It was in this context that Richard Elderfield's lilac icon made its appearance amid a glow of national pride and many media fanfares, including a brief BMC film which summed up the Minor 1000's appeal. A radiant middle-class family, husband and wife with older son and younger daughter, marvel in clipped tones at Richard's car in its salad days, freshly off the assembly line and exhibited in state at a motor show under spotlights and surrounded by plastic chain link fencing. The husband divides his spaniel-like gaze between his wife and the car, before saying: 'Bill Anderson tells me the Minor's the best car he ever had. Marvellous on corners. Bags of power. Miles and miles per gallon too.' His wife responds: 'Jane took me to dine at Heal's. We sailed through the traffic and parked just like that.' Boy does a 'Cor – a million' riff, referring to his school chums' excitement about a million of anything, and Girl has a doll's-house enthusiasm for the amount of room beneath the boot for luggage. In less than two minutes of black-and-white film, the apogee of the Morris Minor's appeal is gloriously summed up.

How different was the fate that awaited this very car, overturned on a Welsh lane and stashed in a barn with the brown mud of Carmarthenshire pasted all over its garishly repainted red bodywork. But in the hands of Richard Elderfield a marvellous resurrection has very slowly taken place, which really began after a dinner-party conversation with Enoch Powell. In his role as regional chairman of a professional marketing association, Elderfield hosted a dinner in Coventry at which the Conservative MP was guest speaker and therefore sat beside him during the meal. Politics was a rather dicey subject at the time, particularly where Powell was concerned, and Elderfield introduced the subject of his Morris Minor. It was then that he learned the significance of the numberplate, Powell being a Greek scholar who naturally seized on BMC's learned extra for its millionth car.

'It could have been MHU, as it is, or MU, which is the alternative spelling for a million in Greek,' he told his host.

'MU 1? Now that really would be worth something,' exclaimed Elderfield. (It took Powell, who was less interested in football than Classics, a moment or two to catch on.)

Sitting at home surrounded by a suitcase-full of photographs and documents about the unique car, Richard and Neil look like the very picture of Morris Minor enthusiasts. But they are not – or at least weren't, until the pleasures and obligations of owning the millionth car became unavoidable. Richard still ponders over the gentle pace of the rescue operation, in a voice which unmistakeably links him to Birmingham after years of exile working on the south coast.

It's funny, really, there were all the 'car people' looking for the millionth Minor and in some cases thinking that they had it, and here's me all the time, a businessman who's not really interested in cars, and I had it all along.

At one time there was even an attempt by someone else to register the number MHU 1 on another car, presumably a Minor, which led to brief police involvement.

Elderfield didn't have the specialist skills to renovate the car himself but he eventually found a man who did. Derek Smith lectured in engineering and bodywork repair at Norbrook College, on the picturesque campus at Shoreham-on-Sea airfield where light aircraft buzz in and out against a backdrop of Lancing public school's colossal pseudo-Gothic chapel: a scene straight from Biggles or Bulldog Drummond. Three train stops along from Angmering, the college was handy and full of mechanical expertise. Another much larger renovation project was under way there on a similar unhurried schedule: the restoration of a 1958 Bristol *Britannia* passenger airliner. Smith's first reaction to the prospect of working on a Minor Million was typical, because he knew about the original colour. 'When first seen,' he summarised, 'it makes one violently sick.' Paintwork restoration was fortunately almost the last task for the team, who laboured for five years on the old car in between their normal curriculum demands. Traditional lead solder was used to repair parts of the frame, several new panels were moulded and cut, and original parts were tracked down to replace defunct or rusted ones. Elderfield had meanwhile chatted about the project at Angmering golf course to John Cooper, whose partnership with BMC produced the legendary Mini Cooper. He kept his own big car collection nearby at Ferring and lent his expertise. Then the car travelled north and west past its old home in the chicken shed near Birmingham to a specialist company in Telford who finished things off.

Meanwhile the Elderfields had become intrigued by the world of Morris Million enthusiasts, a microcosm of the large and flourishing Morris Minor Owners Club. Research by these other Million owners and devotees had produced a definitive history of many of the 350 special-issue cars. 'Look at this one,' says Richard, brandishing a tragic photograph of No. 1,000,343 plunged bonnet first into a swamp at Fige Farm at Malagash in Nova Scotia. 'When they published that in the Million Club magazine in 1995 you could have her free, provided you sorted out collection. No doubt someone's done her up by now.' The wreck was one of 31 Millions which went overseas, leaving 319 for the home market of the United Kingdom and Ireland. Another Million, No. 1,000,259, was rusting to dust in a field at Linicro in Skye according to Elderfield's yellowing edition of the club magazine, which reckoned her too far gone even thirteen years ago. There were worries about a third in Norway. But many others were as resplendent as the one sunning itself on the gravel outside the room where we were poring over the old papers. Indeed the closest relative to the Elderfields' precious car, No. 1,000,001, was pictured beautifully restored and garaged in a loving home at Silverado in California.

Elderfield got to know some of the owners, including his fellow businessman Andrew Dyer, managing director in the south of England for Stagecoach, who bought his Million twenty-three years ago, when he was issued with his first company car. 'For the first time I could spend a bit extra on my fun car, and I saw this ad in the local Cheltenham paper, placed by a woman who had inherited her Million from her mother.' Like so many Minor enthusiasts, Dyer had grown up with one – his grandparents' – and graduated to an ordinary Minor of his own in the 1970s. He knew that Millions were a bit special. The one he bought had only 17,000 miles on the clock, and he has been sparing in his own use of it, adding another 30,000-odd miles. But that has included memorable trips to Brittany, the Loire and almost as far as Strasbourg, as well as Cornwall and Scotland. Dyer likes the thought, when motoring by Million round the UK, that wherever he happens to be, one of the car's 319 home-market relations will have started its working life nearby. 'BMC deliberately distributed them all over the country, from Jersey to Shetland,' he says – another piece of Million history which the Owners' Club has nailed. He also enjoys the comments he gets.

> The French generally think it's just another eccentric English car, but you get two distinct reactions here in England. Young people tend to ask, 'Why did you paint it that revolting colour?' Older ones, particularly in Oxford where I used to live, say, 'Is that really a Morris Million?'

The car has let him down only once, when it grumbled to a halt with a cracked rotor arm.

News of the restoration of the millionth Minor spread gradually, especially after a local TV documentary, which also introduced the Elderfields to other exotic owners. A generous slice in a national BBC tribute to the Morris Minor kept the interest coming. Richard found himself in an exclusive group that included such determined enthusiasts as Paul and Audrey Gelinas, Americans in their country's diplomatic corps, who hunted down No. 1,000,156 in Stevenage. It had travelled 104,000 miles by then in the hands of eight owners, but none of them lived any further from Stevenage than Harrow. That was all to change. The lilac lovely was shipped shortly afterwards to Mexico City, where the Gelinases were posted to the US embassy. They hosted a Morris Minor lunch not long afterwards and learned from a waitress that there was another Morris Million already in the city ('No one, señor, could mistake that mauve').

Other owners have included John Rolfe, an agricultural engineer in the Cambridgeshire fens, with ten other Minors in his collection and a thick skin when it comes to local comments. Beaming from his lilac cockpit, he has dismissed regular quips that the colour is sissy and girly, and why doesn't he get a matching handbag. Joan Pick of Croydon put up with family jokes about her Purple Vomit after she bought her Million from her parents in 1963, along with a meticulous ledger of all the money they had ever spent on petrol and oil for the car. Her own mileage went down as her social conscience about the environment went up, and eventually she stored the Million in a garage because she couldn't bear the thought of someone scrapping it or using it for stock car racing (it spent its retirement under a drip from the ceiling, which gradually created a small stalagmite on the car's roof). Joan meanwhile went out and got herself a bespoke Geoffrey Butler touring bicycle, and – guess what? – had it painted in authentic BMC Minor Million lilac.

The Morris Million marked the halfway point in the Minor's twenty-four-year production run and came just after the zenith of new versions of the model. Its appearance at the end of 1960 just failed to keep annual sales above 100,000 for a fourth year. They dropped to a little over 95,000, and for the next eleven years were to dwindle steadily until 1971, the final year of production, when only 5,705 were sold. The United States market, which had always faltered, was abandoned altogether in 1962. The car remained vastly popular because of a buoyant second-hand market – the one used by the Cowley workers I met at the Lord Nuffield club – but its days as a new and regularly updated model were numbered. Style, power and above all passenger comfort began to overtake it as surely as the growing number of bigger and smarter cars that whisked past Minors on the roads. The designers did their best: flashing light indicators completely replaced 'flicker' semaphores in 1961, fresh-air heaters and much better windscreen wipers were installed in 1963, the glovebox got a smart new lid in 1964. But the changes were superficial compared with the relative luxuries of Ford's Cortina and Escort, or even the Mini – all of which comfortably topped the Minor's final total sale of 1,619,857 cars.

The Minor's rounded shape had come full circle, from looking dramatically modern compared to the boxy cars of the 1930s to seeming quaintly old-fashioned beside the differently boxy 1960s models, such as the Triumph Herald or Vauxhall Viva. These were faster, too, and not a great deal more expensive. In 1968, when BMC finally decided to phase out the Minor 1000 and produce the new Marina instead, the Mini undercut the Minor by £438 to £476 (£5,250 and £5,700 today) and was infinitely more Sixties and cool. Its laurels were more important than the Minor's to Issigonis, who was now Sir Alec and in retirement, although he never lost interest in car design or the smaller mechanical challenges of the miniature steam trains which he made in his spare time. He did not want to play a practical part any more in the changing trends of motoring, commenting waspishly:

> The modern car is much too sophisticated for my liking because I still enjoy driving without being surrounded by an environment of domestic and household appliances.

He was also quoted as saying that ideally the drivers of his cars should be kept alert by sitting on a bed of nails. Production of the zestiest of his Minors, the 1000 convertible, stopped in midsummer 1969, with the last saloons coming off the Cowley assembly lines in November the following year. The remaining 5,705 were Travellers and commercial Minors — vans and pick-ups. Poignantly, these included final attempts at modernity in an oil-level warning light on the dashboard and, in a small number of 1971 cars, an alternator instead of the traditional old dynamo.

And now here is Richard Elderfield's memento of the Minor's headiest days, beautiful but lifeless on a gravel drive in Sussex. What awaits? He has tried to interest museums, but so far none have been in a position to pay, and he cannot afford to donate a car on which he has lavished so much care and funds. The British Motor Museum at Gaydon might be interested in taking the car on loan, particularly after several outings by MHU 1 this year to events connected with the sixtieth anniversary of the Morris Minor. But I got the impression that a buyer with upwards of £15,000 and a taste for lilac would get a fair hearing in Angmering. After nearly forty years, there could soon be another name in that historic register book. There would certainly be a market.

However, although the Minor's 'official' production life ended in 1971, the car was soon to stage a remarkable re-appearance, and not just as a classic collector's marque. To check this out, I had to take another train, this time to Bristol and Bath.

Chapter 5
Charlie and the Minor Factory

Eat your heart out, Henry Ford! The car of the 1980s is the elderly Morris Minor.

Nigel Bunyan, *Bristol Evening Post*, 1978

 I WAS LUCKY IN THE TIME and place of my first real job. Bath in the early 1970s was a golden, mellow, semi-ruinous city with a cast of local characters who seemed to a cub reporter to be in a similar state. There was Charmian Deckers, the former model for Balenciaga, and her daughter Nina Sanctuary, who rented me a basement; the writer Angela Carter, who was said to get undressed for bed with the curtains open in her own basement just up the hill; Gilbert Young, whose crusade for World Government was global in aim but relentlessly focused on the *Bath and West Evening Chronicle*, on which I was the junior trainee; a man with an enormous exploded diagram of a pig's insides which he brought into our messy, gossipy office and unrolled all over my desk (everyone else had mysteriously left the room) to explain his cure for swine vesicular disease.

It was my job to explore these people, and I loved it. But there was someone on the *Chron* who was much better at the work than I was; a saturnine man in a black leather jacket called Edward Goring who wrote the paper's diary column 'Day by Day'. As happens in Britain's regional media, especially those parts of it based in beautiful places, he was many times overqualified for a modest evening paper with sales of around 35,000 a night. A refugee from the *Daily Mail* in London, he brought all the skills of that newspaper to bear on the social life of Bath. Nightclubs and restaurants were made or broken by him. He mixed easily with the lords and ladies who maintained, in a ropy but appealing way, the social traditions established in eighteenth-century Bath by Beau Nash. And he discovered the story of Charlie Ware and the Morris Minor Factory.

Ware was already a fixture in 'Day by Day' when I arrived in Bath. A charming young art-college lecturer, he was doing up a house in Royal Crescent and making an interesting and largely convincing case that a property developer could be good for the world and fun too. He was friends with the inspired clowns of Bath Arts Workshop and the Natural Theatre Company, who were trying out their street theatre in this gentle backwater before making a success of it all over the world. You may remember their star performer, Ralph Oswick, leading the Millennium procession up The Mall dressed as a bulky matron with a pram. Ware bought an enormous hotel which no one else wanted in Great Pulteney Street (where house prices are now in the millions of pounds) and rented it to hippies during one of those languorous summer festivals when the sun rose again almost immediately after setting, and the sky over Bath seemed permanently full of hot air balloons. He marched in step with the Bath Preservation Trust and got on with their largely conventional and respectable membership too. They all wanted to save the most beautiful city in England.

Ware had a natural eye for beauty, especially in landscape and design. He was born in another lovely city, Edinburgh, the son of two artists who gave him a properly unconventional upbringing. While his mother painted at home, his father taught art at Fettes public school, *alma mater* of former Prime Minister Tony Blair but in those days a thoroughly conservative institution. Ware senior reacted against its restrictive traditions with brio, and Charlie remembers him as 'a violent pacifist vegetarian' who enjoyed his licence to subvert the political opinions of the young Scottish rich. His pacifism was put to the most serious test possible when Charlie was four, and the Second World War broke out with Hitler's invasion of Poland. His father worked on the land for the duration, and Charlie recalls with wistful pleasure: 'We moved around the country in a succession of damp but picturesque cottages, surrounded by the smell of oil paints. I'm grateful to have been spared any great love for middle-class suburbia.' His mother also gave him a lifelong affection for nettle soup.

It was a natural progression for Charlie to the Slade School of Fine Art in London, where he qualified and was then taken on to teach etching. He had a mastery of line and the sort of quick thinking which makes for effective sketches. Only a little older than many of his students, he

shared their sense of fun and naturally gravitated to
Bohemian areas in Camden and Islington, then run-down in
a way unimaginable today, but cheap and lively places to
live. Lively but threatened. Bulldozers were moving in, and
Charlie reacted with a milder version of his father's
furiously-held opinions: an enthusiastic belief that the lines
of Georgian terraces could be saved.

> I had always liked buildings. Whenever we passed a church
> on a family outing, my Dad would stop and have a good look
> round. I inherited his feel for them, and I knew that the
> houses in north London were much too well-built to throw
> away.

Promotion in the art world took him to a lecturing post
at Corsham Court, the graceful Somerset mansion which
had recently been given by its cultured owner Lord
Methuen to Bath Academy of Art. Ware's salary now gave
him enough to buy his first dirt-cheap house back in
Islington and to start a painstaking restoration, the first of
many. He soon realised one of the principles of property
development: that buying houses and repairing them in
itself creates further demand. Business prospered so much
that he abandoned art teaching and extended his renovation
empire to Bath, a golden plum for a man with his talents.
House after house stood forlornly empty in the early 1970s
(I remember writing in the *Chronicle* about several whose
owners simply couldn't be traced and others which gave up
the struggle and quietly collapsed), and almost all were

potentially Grade One listed buildings. Charlie bought one in Rivers Street for £800, and, like a beneficent cure, the Ware Effect crept up the hills; blackened terraces were stone-washed, rotten window wood recarpentered. What remained of Kingsmead Square after the wartime Baedeker Raids in April 1942 became a template for successful renovation in the most unpromising circumstances, and other developers joined in.

'For about seven years I was very, very rich,' says Ware, who himself then lived in a hundred sumptuous acres at Battlefields, two miles from Bath's northern rim, another congregating point for hippy veterans of 1960s summers of love. Rumours of colourful goings-on drew me regularly as a reporter to the many rickety outbuildings where, later, the Brinks MAT robbery gang were to smelt in secret much of the £26 million they stole from Heathrow in 1983. Ware had long gone by then. In his day it was a top *Chronicle* hunting ground for nothing more serious than free-love nests and cannabis plantations, and even these were more imagined than real.

'Champagne Charlie' as the *News of the World* was about to dub him, presided over this benign little planet, as well as a large house in the Royal Crescent, the most prestigious address in Bath, and his Georgian mansion in Islington which would now be worth millions of pounds. His portfolio of properties bought to renovate swelled and became ever more ambitious, with Bath's Theatre Royal adding a non-residential side whose potential profits were unclear, although Ware's revival of its programme helped Roxy

Music get started. He was overextended, and such exposure would be fatal if the property market faltered and the banks called time. It did, they did, and in a few short weeks in 1974 Ware lost everything except a final debt of just under £1,000,000.

It was just before then that I left Bath to work in Bradford, and my contact with Ware dwindled to reading occasional newspaper articles about him in what, for me, became a very Yorkshire-centred world. I knew in general terms that he had staged a business comeback and that it was based on Morris Minors. But Penny and I had sold ours by then and moved on to the revolutionary comforts of a second-hand Vauxhall Astra (a car, incidentally, which celebrated its ten millionth sale in May 2008 without winning any of the affection lavished on the Minor). The subject settled in some backwater of my mind – until the task of exploring the Minor's biography brought Ware immediately to mind. He must be over seventy by now, I reckoned. Could he still be in business? Just one phone call and I was on the train to Bristol and Charlie's Morris Minor Centre on Brislington Trading Estate.

You know when you approach a beehive or a wasps' nest? Suddenly there are identical small insects everywhere in numbers you never see in the world at large. Ditto Brislington. The line of parked Morris Minors starts well down from Charlie's office and garage unit; his forecourt is jammed with them, and there are dozens more inside and parked nose to tail in the back yard. This is where hundreds of Morris Minors go to live, not to die – so Charlie explained to me over an egg-and-beans lunch in the local greasy spoon, where dozens of his cars (he borrows whichever one he feels like over the lunch break) are familiar in the car park. First, though, he had to finish taking a Minor-struck young couple round the workshop where his twenty staff were welding, spraying and wiring a range of half-gutted cars that customers had sent for renovation or Charlie had simply found.

He murmurs superlatives about one handsome saloon which the couple seem smitten by. 'We have all the spares,' he says like a reassuring doctor, conducting them into a warehouse section lined with shelves of brown boxes labelled British Leyland, BMC, Morris and Austin. The mechanics are meanwhile brewing up on a stove which has just been heating glue to seal internal panels. We get diverted into a discussion of a bright red ex-Royal Mail Minor 1000 van, which had special extra locks fitted to its doors to guard the post. There's an interesting glass case, too, with Minor souvenirs, original brochures, a bottle of Moggy Ale and, under an exhibition bell jar, a model by a man in Birmingham who will make you a miniature scene of your Minor outside your front door. Another picture shows envelopes that have challenged the Post Office over the years – addressed to 'The Morris Minor Man, England' or 'The builder of Morris Minors who appeared on the Pebble Mill programme'.

Then Charlie is free, and for the first time in twenty-five years I am back in a Morris Minor – as soon as the engine growls into life the 1970s return. The nostalgia is overwhelming; the solid clunk of the door closing, the sense of being inside a can. The car shakes in the old familiar way, like a wet dog, as we bounce over a kerb and proceed round the industrial estate to the caff. The road winds but Charlie has a way of driving in a straight line, like a slower version of a Formula One driver gaining fractions of a second by cutting bends. He was never dangerous, but being in a Morris Minor certainly helped. Drivers coming the other way looked forgiving, and in several cases smiled to see a dear old Moggy. Some of them probably knew Charlie but I am sure that others assumed he was a retired vicar or the equivalent of an elderly, Morris-Minor-owning relative of their own.

Plates clean, we settled down over large, companionable mugs of tea, and Charlie took up where we had left off.

> The recession wiped me out. I had guarantees on property of £10 million but this was like Northern Rock; it was the last big banking crisis. I suppose I could have got out in time and gone to Jersey and stored away what I had like a squirrel, but I didn't believe in that. I wanted to stay in Bath, and I wanted to earn my own living.

He was forty-one and had a young family whose needs led him, reluctantly, to sign on and get benefit payments for six weeks. But he was also tough. Before the Slade, he had done national service, including a spell in Cyprus, where he saw action against General Grivas's EOKA separatists. He was a popular bankrupt, whose friends did not desert him. But while they were offering to help tide him over, he started making his own plans. Most days, he dropped in at a wine bar in St Margaret's Buildings where his old pals hung out, to network and look for opportunities. Rather to his surprise, the first and best one came from the husband of the laid-back woman who ran the place. 'He was a Charlie Drake type of person,' Ware recalls. 'A car dealer. He took me to the big car sales in Westbury and that's where I got started.'

The two Charlies came back with a couple of old crocks, bought for a song, and got them back into some sort of roadworthy shape on a patch of land that the wine-bar husband owned in the hippy corner of Bath, Walcot. Ware wasn't allowed to run a business, as an undischarged bankrupt, so his new friend looked after the books, and his wife Bunny signed cheques. Gradually a little enterprise grew, sown with a couple of £200 loans (£1,500 each today) from friends. 'Within a year,' says Charlie, 'I'd paid off all my local debts, except for one.' That was for a slap-up meal at Bath's most celebrated restaurant of the time, The Hole in the Wall. He reckoned that George Perry Smith, its owner (and his fellow star of Ed Goring's column in the 'Champagne Charlie' days) could afford the loss.

The business grew modestly and moved to bigger premises in London Road, taking in unloved cars and getting them back in action. Charlie noticed how regularly Morris Minors came in, and one day he realised that there were eight in his yard. He was taking night-school classes in car maintenance, and he got to know the different Minor engines, seeking out cutaway diagrams and researching their history. Out for a spin in one of the cars, he found himself comparing it to the Georgian properties whose restoration had made his first fortune. They were elegant and practical examples of design, and so was the Morris Minor. It also required much less outlay.

> To make a house complete, you need enormous reserves of capital. To make a car complete, you don't. If you keep a well-made machine and maintain it, the cost is almost infinitely low. I drove back to the yard thinking, 'There could be a very good business here.'

It was a significant moment for the second life of the Morris Minor. In the course of researching this book, I have met people with different opinions about the quality of 'Charlie Ware Jobs', and quite a few who added vigorous adjectives to their admission of what a new or renovated Minor from his centre costs. But there is no doubting the effect of an article by Ed Goring in his 'Day by Day' column in the *Evening Chronicle* in November 1976. It can claim credit for kick-starting an existing but modest revival of interest in Sir Alec Issigonis's inspirational car:

> Chares Ware, who went bankrupt by cornering the property market in Bath, is now earning a living by cornering the market in Morris Minors. Bulbous nose to bustle tail, there are now more than 60 of them crammed on a newly-acquired site in Lower Bristol Road, newly labelled the Morris Minor Centre.

Journalism in Britain works from the bottom up, and within days the *Sunday Mirror*'s motoring correspondent Roy Spicer had picked up on Ed's piece (probably sold it by one of the *Chronicle*'s veteran reporters who made money on the side via such tips). More significantly, *Sunday Times* special correspondent Ian Nairn came to Bath and wrote a piece under the headline 'The Morris Minor Rides Again.' He was enraptured by the complete contrast between glossy new-car showrooms and Charlie's scruffy yard sandwiched between the Bristol Road and a viaduct carrying Isambard Kingdom Brunel's Great Western Railway. As the then new high-speed trains swished above the old but doughty cars, and Charlie sorted himself another roll-up, Nairn wrote: 'It looks like one of those garages deep in the Auvergne where mechanics perform miracles and then go off to a splendid Routier-type lunch.'

By coincidence, at around this time I had every reason to be grateful to Ian Nairn for a piece he wrote supporting a battle I was involved in, to save the dilapidated but handsome square in Manningham, Bradford, where I lived in a house I had bought for £1,800. The council wanted to bulldoze it, as they so often did in those days, but Nairn's piece was instrumental in stopping them in their tracks. It was read, and acted upon, by every conservation guru from the Civic Trust to the Victorian Society. His comparably impassioned article on Charles Ware's Morris Minors was read by BBC producers at Pebble Mill in Birmingham, who followed in his footsteps to Lower Bristol Road. In the nine months after this double whammy of the *Sunday Times* and daytime TV, Charlie received more than ten thousand inquiries about buying or restoring cars.

Thus began the heyday of the Revived Minor. Demand and supply were dramatically reversed, and Charlie began to scour the country for unwanted cars.

> I know England extremely well through Morris Minors, and it's wonderful how they conform to all the clichéd ideas people have about them. Go up a little valley . . . there's a little house with roses round the door, and there's the Morris sitting in the drive. People never throw them away – even today, I still find them in barns.

He scans the internet for house-contents sales, especially in the country, and keeps his local contacts sweet.

> I think I pay fair prices; certainly in a lot of places I'm offering at least a third more than any local buyer would. There's a place in South Wales where I go and pick up a Minor year after year. The phone rings and a voice asks: 'Is that Mr Ware? See, I have a little Morris.' . . . I'm known as the mad bugger who'll pay all this money for an old car.

Buying the worn-out Moggies can be emotional, though. Charlie dealt with an elderly woman in Devon who asked him to find a buyer as far away as possible, because she would be upset if she was reminded of happy motoring days by seeing the car in someone else's hands. He sold it in Essex, but admits to an uneasy feeling that the buyer might well have been thinking of retiring to the country – in Devon.

Another seller, a retired squadron leader with a DFC and bar who had braved Nazi bombers in the Battle of Britain, had tears in his eyes when he parted with his Traveller. The same strong feelings possess many of Ware's other clients, who have brought their Morris Minors to Bath, and now Bristol, over the years to have them renovated rather than sold. One customer, whose Minor was stripped down, cleaned and rebored, wanted to see every part.

> He helped us strip the engine down, watched as we welded things and then helped put it all back together again. Another dear regular arrives here for services after driving down the M4 from Newbury, perched on a tasselled cushion so that she can see between the top of the steering wheel and the dashboard. 'I've never taken Bessie over 45 mph, Mr Ware,' she often says. Over the years we have had lots of people selling us Minors simply because we'll find them a good home. It's like horses; they know we won't be sending them to Belgium to be made into soup.

As a result, exceptional cars come his way. In 1978 when the editor of the *American Morris Minor Owners' Magazine* called by, Charlie had just taken delivery of an elderly woman's flawless white 1965 saloon with only fifteen thousand miles on the clock. That sort of thing has happened regularly since.

Thirty years' experience of dealing with Morris Minors

has convinced Ware that people who like them are likeable themselves; the car is classless in his experience, with owners coming from country mansions and council estates. 'It's a friendly car, and it's got this friendly face, with the lidded headlamp eyes and smiling radiator mouth. Everyone has happy memories of the Morris Minor.' Most of the ones who come to Brislington also want to share it. 'Out comes the dreaded wallet,' says Charlie, whose works rivalled some of the major local tourist attractions when he was in Bath, 'and they lovingly go through at least forty-eight photographs of their car.' Scribbled notes are pressed into his hand with website addresses on Facebook or YouTube, which is chock-a-block with films of Morris Minors doing everything from taking people shopping to plunging through Canadian snowdrifts. He loves it really, but it takes time.

Ware's admiration for the practical side of the car's design grew as more and more different Minors arrived at Lower Bristol Road. Gradually he gained personal experience of everything from the first MM models of 1948 to the final batch of pick-ups and vans which left British Leyland at Cowley in 1971. He had kept up with his classy Bath friends throughout his financial rollercoaster, and it was through one of them, the engineer and inventor Jeremy Fry, that he eventually met Sir Alec Issigonis. The two of them went to Birmingham with Lord Snowdon, also a friend of Fry's, for a session photographing the great man at the wheel of a Minor. One of the prints hangs on the wall in Charlie's office at Brislington.

He came back to Bath more certain than ever that the Minor had a more fundamental future than just becoming a classic car with the appeal of anything historic that still works. Fetching another mug of tea, he says:

> It is a classic, but in a different sense. It is a classic piece of design because it works so well and so simply. You can teach yourself quite easily to look after the engine, well beyond the basic standbys like using a stocking if the fanbelt goes. Even the electrics are very simple.

Of course, the Charles Ware Morris Minor Centre would be happy to do the work for you, and the same simplicities work very well for them. Ware is a businessman, and his joy at discovering the Minor as a way of reviving his fortunes had a sound financial side. The last Morris Minors to be sold new went for £737 and, with six years' depreciation at least, by the time they reached Charlie were worth a couple of hundred or so. But he found that a restored car fetched a minimum of £600, and very soon more. By the time Ian Nairn wrote his *Sunday Times* piece in August 1977, saloons from Lower Bristol Road were costing £750 to around £1,100, and convertibles and Travellers between £875 and £1,300. Nairn took his own eight-year-old convertible, XPC 359G, in for renovation and paid £575 for a thorough makeover, including a new bonnet, partial engine rebuild and underseal. In 1978 the Minor was dropped from the actuarial tables in the motor trade's price Bible, *Glass's Guide*, because its cost was disobeying all the rules. By the end of the year, Ware's Travellers were fetching £3,000, and cars for renovation were pouring in, including one owned by one of the Queen's chauffeurs.

What was happening? The answer was a surge of excitement among Minor owners – and fanciers – that their much-loved Old Reliables were not yet doomed to become a rare breed, with the usual classic-car problems of finding interested mechanics and spares. The strength of feeling was remarkable, and it had the personal edge which has always attached to the Minor. Right at the start of its career *Autocar*'s road tester had written presciently after the 1948 Motor Show:

> Now and again it happens that circumstances bring a person suddenly into prominence, and he or she instantly becomes a favourite in the public affections. Something similar occurs with new cars, and it is likely to happen to the new Morris Minor.

Thirty years later, the same magazine paid an enthusiastic visit to Lower Bristol Road and concluded: 'Owners of this utilitarian but captivating little car are refusing to allow it to die.' Ware's initiative was greeted with similar gutsy descriptions in a splash of media coverage, not just in Britain but internationally. Roy Spicer's *Daily Mirror* piece set the tone: 'The old girl has style all right – she looks cuddly, moves well and still has a fantastic number of admirers.' The Australian Associated Press described 'the Mighty Minor, very much alive and kicking', *Die Welt* called Ware's cars 'classless and beloved', and the *Daily Express* celebrated 'the world's favourite old banger, coming back in style'. The moody, strike-beset atmosphere of James Callaghan's last years as Prime Minister helped. Margaret Thatcher's bracing tenure of Downing Street was still a year away, and it was still customary to talk down the country, including the bland and undistinguished cars being made by British Leyland. Oh, said philosophers in countless bars, why ever did they axe the good old Morris Minor?

Ware's second great business revelation was the abundance of spares. He checked carefully before deciding on the Minor as the sole focus of his business and found that almost everything, from windscreen wipers to grease nipples, was still available from BL. The company had a stockpile of body parts, and there were also so many Morris Minors coming into the Bath workshop that unrepairable wrecks could be cannibalised at the rate of five a week. Up and up went the prices; Travellers had doubled to £6,000 by 1981, when turnover at Lower Bristol Road topped £500,000 for the year. Up went the workforce, too. Ware's staff had started only with his wife Bunny, who was unaffected by the bankruptcy and legally allowed to be a director, and their long-standing pal from building-renovation days, Sebastian Beazeley, a man half-hidden by wild hair and beard who much appealed to photographers when the media discovered the Morris Minor boom. By 1981 there were twenty-eight on the payroll, including twenty-two-year-old Clare Cross, who also had long hair, but young and golden, and appeared in renewed press photographs accompanied by puns. They got her to strip out seats and adjust the interior trim.

No one enjoys a monopoly of new business for long unless they can patent it, and Ware's initiative was rapidly followed by other Morris Minor specialists all over Britain. There were some who predated Bath, usually in the hands of quiet, highly-skilled mechanics content with a modest turnover and focused on really high-quality work. But, as Charlie had shown – and as he kept telling journalists, who faithfully repeated his words – the Minor was a simple challenge for anyone with a basic knowledge of cars. By the mid-1980s most owners or would-be buyers had a Morris Minor specialist with an hour or two's drive of their home, even if quality was patchy. One of Ware's sound bites was telling, and has occasionally been flung back in his face by customers unhappy with his own work or its cost: 'It's the last of the nuts and bolts cars. It can be serviced by an idiot.'

To keep ahead of the game, he extended his Minor services. You could buy your own components from him – a hood for £100, for example, or new seasoned-ash timber for a Traveller – and later on a facsimile of the original manual, postcards of Minors in action and other bric-a-brac. He developed good links with British Leyland and helped to persuade them to keep manufacturing some Minor parts, which could be used by other cars in the firm's fleet. (As a result, said the *Sunday Times* in 1980, it was easier to get bits and bobs for a Minor from BL than a new door handle for a Mini.) He became adept at fitting different engines and gearboxes taken from other, more modern makes of car. In the meanwhile his touch with the media did not desert him. In 1983 the centre teamed up with *The Sun*, Britain's highest-circulation newspaper then as now, to offer a free Morris Minor as a competition prize. It was a 1970 Clipper Blue saloon with a book value of £3,500. But, as *The Sun* inimitably said: 'You can't put a price on the Minor magic.' And another tag – better said than read – alluded to current industrial troubles in proclaiming the car 'The only Minor in Britain that won't go on strike.'

Shortly after the centrespread appeared, Ware made an interesting venture into the conventional car sales market. A Ford dealer from London, Michael Molloy, visited Bath, partly to see what all the fuss was about, and partly because his wife, son and daughter had all separately told him that, whatever the delights of Ford Escorts and Fiestas, the runabout they all really wanted was a second-hand Morris Minor. 'I realised that there must be a market,' he said, and before the year was out he was offering a limited range of Minors at his garage in Woolwich. He took two apprentice fitters on under the then Government's Youth Opportunities Scheme to learn their trade on the simple vehicles and told the *Daily Express* that turnover was around £14,000 a month. Restored convertibles were costing up to £7,000 and were becoming, in Molloy's words, almost too hot to handle. He had been converted himself. 'Many of us now drive Morris Minors,' he said, 'and therefore happily practise what we preach.'

A second, similar operation opened as a Ware franchise at a BL dealer in Newcastle upon Tyne, but Ware's hopes that these would be the first of at least ten licensed outlets were not realised, and plenty of his other ambitious dreams have yet to be fulfilled. In particular, his hopes for a new production line of Morris Minors adapted for the twenty-first century are still just hopes – though, as we shall see later on, they may yet come to play a part in the future, and wider, story of car manufacturing. Back in the 1970s and 1980s Ware had one other fundamental effect on the Morris Minor itself, by increasing the old car's profile and encouraging its restoration.

Just as the chronology of chicken and egg has never been decided, it is impossible to say whether Ware was crucial to organised Morris Minor enthusiasm or *vice versa*. In any event, the simultaneous discovery of something new is a frequent phenomenon and a feature of many inventions, from photography to proportional representation. A panel-beater and sprayer in Scunthorpe, Tom Newton, had three Minors: a very early convertible from 1949 and two saloons made in 1950 and 1955. And it was in 1976, the same year that Charlie Ware started his Bath centre, that Tom Newton and some friends got together and launched a club for Morris Minor owners. Within a year, the club had a hundred members, including some in Australia, Sweden and France. Its mission was to keep as many Minors on the road as possible, and it was to become spectacularly successful at achieving it. By 1986 the British Morris Minor Owners' Club (MMOC) had over forty branches or affiliated societies and some 6,500 members. Today, there are some 15,000 members in Britain alone and a calendar of events that would leave the busiest socialite whacked.

The British have always been good at organising themselves into clubs to promote particular interests or enthusiasms, and the Morris Minor was an ideal subject. There were cars to buy and sell, wrecks to report, research to be done, money to be raised for other good causes. The main club soon became an umbrella for local branches and established friendly links with more specialist Minor clubs, for owners or admirers of ex-Government vehicles, the Morris Million, or people with a thing about vans.

There was even, for a time, a Society for the Prevention of Cruelty to Morris Minors, started by an accountant from Cheshire, Dave Plant. Several hundred Minor partisans signed up and received curiosities such as a member's vow:

> I do solemnly swear to keep, love and cherish thee as long as we both shall live, to polish, pamper and maintain thee to a standard becoming and deserving of a car of such quality, character and charm.

This was essentially a bit of fun for Plant, but nearer to the feelings of some Minor owners than he perhaps imagined. John Wright from Derby claimed to sweep his drive every time he took out his two-door saloon, originally bought for £75 from a scrapyard called (inappropriately in his car's case) Journey's End. Bert Brett of Abercanaid, near Glamorgan, phoned the weatherman before journeys in his Traveller and claimed that he had been caught by rain only once in seven years of using the car. He kept it in a carpeted garage, wore white gloves when adjusting the engine and persuaded his wife Elsie to wear special soft shoes when she came along as a passenger. Still more extreme, a pensioner from Tiverton called Reg Day attempted to arrange for his Morris Minor to be buried with him after his death. He admitted that for thirty-one years, he had put the car before his wife Sylvia. Sadly, the burial authorities turned him down.

Such extreme Minoristas certainly did their best to live out the SPCMM's vow, but the great majority of Morris Minor owners have been thoroughly practical, and as a result have got things done. For several years the MMOC has been entrusted with an important part in the City of London's Lord Mayor's Parade, and it did a brilliant job in choreographing the Dance of the Minors, which was one of the most memorable moments of the 2000 Manchester Commonwealth Games. Its current secretary is Ray Newell, who has written more copiously and knowledgably about the Morris Minor than anyone else in the world, and its finances have been so prudently conducted that in 1996 it was able to spend £58,000 on a modern HQ at the Sir Francis Ley industrial park in Derby. Sir Francis would have been delighted. He was a Victorian industrialist whose Vulcan works in Derby exported iron-based goods throughout the world, and he was also a notable enthusiast – for baseball. He served on the Baseball Council, which introduced America's national game to Britain, and his firm's recreation ground was for decades one of its few strongholds.

I do not think that there is anything related to Morris Minors that the MMOC has not done, including the commissioning of a limited edition of gold-plated model Moggies to celebrate the car's fiftieth birthday in 1998. The briefest visit to the club's website reveals a world of scholarship and persistence which university departments would envy. Just take a couple of examples from the Scrapyard section of the bulletin board, on which club members report on a constant watch for abandoned Minors. On 16 April 2007 a member with the username Matt reported a split-screen two-door tucked in the corner of a scrapyard at Pease Pottage. 'It is extremely rotten,' he said, adding expertly that the front subframe had come from an Austin Allegro and noting that purple furry covers for the headrests were still inside. By June, the man who sent the car for scrap had come forward, with contacts and a raft of details for any Minor fan with time and patience to attempt a rescue. 'P.S.,' he added, 'I should have saved the purple furry headlining.' Similarly, a rusting Minor hadn't been left for long within sight of the M6 near Manchester's Trafford Park shopping centre before a spotter was keying in the details to the bulletin board. Hey presto! A saviour was rapidly on the scene and posted a courteous note of thanks: 'Hi there. Just thought I would let you know that the Moggy is no longer homeless. She is all wrapped up, and when I'm ready she will be carefully taken apart. Thanks for the tip-off and the directions.'

The bulletin boards are also one of the busiest places for pilgrims seeking the answer to the Legend of the Last Morris

Minor. Rather like *The Da Vinci Code* – a film, incidentally, in which a very smart pale blue Traveller makes a brief appearance behind Tom Hanks and Audrey Tautou – the story is compelling. Did British Leyland make one last Minor in 1974 out of spare parts? And was it, as is usually claimed, for a vicar? Research continues by Minorites everywhere, and they are marvellous people. I was about to meet some, on a bracing day at the edge of the North Yorkshire Moors national park.

Sir Alec Issigonis, creator of the Minor. He was more English than the English thanks to a strongly Anglophile upbringing in Smyrna, now Izmir, in Turkey. *Getty Images*

Issigonis sketched designs on everything from cigarette cartons to the Morris factory floor. In this drawing, the Minor has almost reached its final shape. *PA Photos*

Stealing the Motor Show: the Minor was a sensation at Earl's Court in 1948, drawing bigger crowds than even the sleek XK120 sports car from Jaguar. *Getty Images*

A period advertisement for the Morris Minor, in which the original split screen is seen to good effect. At the time it was 'supreme' in performance and comfort as well as reliability. *Mary Evans Picture Library*

What could be simpler? The dashboard on the Minor allowed few opportunities for a driver to make mistakes. The car was a long-standing favourite for learners (and their instructors). *Alamy*

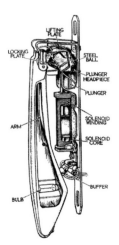

Complete mechanism of the Trafficator, showing the solenoid and the mounting plate. The wire leading from the mounting plate out to the bulb at the tip of the arm can be clearly seen, so that the liability to fracture, owing to the rise and fall of the arm, can be appreciated.

The Minor's original 'trafficator' semaphore indicators used to clunk outwards and upwards with less finesse than this forensic diagram would suggest.

The Morris Traveller, nicknamed the 'Woodie', prompted Dame Edna Everage to remark that even Britain's cars were half-timbered. The model is notorious for wood rot. *Alamy*

Posties drove Minors, as did telephone engineers and the staff of half-a-dozen Government ministries. Military Minors, including Bomb Disposal vans, had four doors for officers, two for other ranks. *The British Postal Museum and Archive*

A Morris Minor police Panda car. Probably not much used for high-speed motorway chases, and strangely enough by the time Regan and Carter of *The Sweeney* needed a car to throw around the streets they preferred a Ford Consul GT. *Rex Features*

Britain's best-known racing driver Stirling Moss did wonders for the Minor's image in the 1950s, as did his rally-driver sister Pat. Both owned beefy, tuned-up models. *Getty Images*

The Minor at the centre of the notorious A6 Murder trial in 1962 which led to the execution of James Hanratty. It was dumped on a pavement in east London after the brutal killing of its owner Michael Gregsten. *Getty Images*

Long hair, long coat, little Minor. Penny Cartledge, now the author's wife, was a typical student owner of the marque in the 1970s. *Martin Wainwright*

One of the best-known of TV drama's many Minors was this Trafalgar Blue model known as Miriam and driven by the rogueish antique dealer Lovejoy, played by Ian McShane. The sporty convertible, or ragtop, fetches some of the highest prices for Minors today. Buyers need to check if the car is an original or a conversion with reinforced bodywork. And the wingnuts on the hood can be a pain. *BBC Photo Library*

Morris and BMC didn't drape minimally-clad women over the Minor. This one got the treatment from local model Jennifer Pietersen at a 60th anniversary rally hosted by Johannesburg's Emerald City casino.

Professor Lobster's marvellous Minor – even the pincers worked. The car's co-creator Phil Vincent used it to go shopping after its TV career ended. Until the police intervened...

The exhibition Abandoned Morris Minors of the West of Ireland helped to make the name of photographer Martin Parr. This - the first amphibious example of the marque - is what happens to Morris Minors when they die.

Martin, Parr, Magnum

Beijing's 2008 Olympics may have put on the ultimate pyrotechnic opening ceremony, but they didn't have a massed ballet of Morris Minors, did they? Manchester's Commonwealth Games did, here photographed by the late Don McPhee, legendary *Guardian* photographer and Morris Minor aficionado.

Don McPhee, courtesy of the Morris Minor Owners Club

The envelope pushed as far as it will go for a Morris Minor rebuild: The Beast, Reading garage-owner Mick Peeling's pride and joy. Gentler devotees of the Minor regularly tell him: 'Oh No! How could you do that to a Moggy?' *Mick Peeling, Morris Minor Centre*

The Archbishop of Canterbury's Minor on its way to 15th place in the Small Car class of the 1980 Himalayan Rally. During its previous 13 years at Lambeth Palace, it had not been allowed out in the rain.

It came second last out of 57 entrants, but Tony Manos's 1951 Minor comfortably finished the London-Dakar World Cup Rally in 2005. *Tony Manos*

Thanks to the Minor's light weight, Manos skimmed over soft sand in the Sahara – most of the time. The following year the car reached Ulan Bator, with the help of fascinated village mechanics in Kazakhstan.
Tony Manos

Inspecting the troops at Farndale on the 2008 charity Daffodil Run of the Bridlington & Wolds Morris Minor Owners' Club. *Martin Wainwright*

The Morris Million limited edition was designed to have a livery, inside and out, which no other car would copy. The commonest nickname for the colour is 'Purple Vomit.' This car is actually the millionth Minor, restored by businessman Richard Elderfield. Enoch Powell commented on its number plate, which is classical Greek for 1 million. *Martin Wainwright*

The natty silver badge in the shape of a Minor door made by John Barker at his workshop in Ugford, near Salisbury. A useful code sign for Minor owners when away from their cars. *Martin Wainwright*

New body shells for the Minor are turned out in Sri Lanka to this day. *Rex Features*

Chapter 6
Mad About the Minor

Morris Minor — never lets you down,
Gets you round the town
Straight from A to B.
Nothing Finer, I don't need to dash
Or to be dead flash,
So that's the car for me.

'The Morris Minor Song',
Morris Minor and the Majors, 1988

 The snow was still lingering on the moor tops above Farndale, but the wild daffodils along the River Dove were out, and so were the Morris Minors. Away in the distance, you could see their hummocky roofs – the yolk of Lord Nuffield's poached egg – just above the hawthorn hedges coming into leaf along the lane into Farndale hamlet. Penny and I had asked permission to park by a cottage because the 'daffodil field' where you usually pay your £2 had been flooded by recent downpours. We told the owner why we had come and pointed out the line of approaching cars. 'Morris Minors?' she said. 'Ooooh, how lovely!'

Within a minute or two, the procession was chuntering past, making that familiar mixture of kittenish growls and popping exhausts which tugs at any Minor-lover's heart. There were only ten or so, but they were polished to a gleaming fault and decorated with yellow ribbons and plastic daffodils, and their drivers looked odd behind the big, high steering wheels because they were wearing yellow stovepipe 'Munchkin' hats. This was the first big outing of the year for Bridlington & Wolds Morris Minor Owners' Club, a Daffodil Rally to raise money for Marie Curie Cancer Care.

The cars had started at Driffield in the drizzle and ploughed on through Malton in torrential rain, but by the time they climbed up on to the North York Moors, the sun was out, and even the open-top beach buggy that had come along too was beginning to dry out. The procession was carefully marshalled on to a patch of hard standing in front of the village hall and the Daffy Caffy, which makes most of its money at this time of year. The car doors opened with the clunk that is as familiar as the growl and pops of the exhaust, and the enthusiasts clambered out.

This was my first chance to meet Morris Minoristas *en masse*, and they did not disappoint me. I recognised their leader at once, Sue Akrill, who features largely on the club's website with her equally enthusiastic husband Chris and their dog Pebbles, the group's mascot. I was hoping to meet Pebbles, who has his own email address and attends such functions as the Barnsley Morris Minor Owners' Club Christmas dinner. But he isn't a rallyer. 'Leave him in the back and he'll chew everything,' says Sue, who runs an ornamental koi carp business and aquatic centre from the Grange at Wansford near Driffield. The tang of leather excites the dog, and Issigonis's door handle loops made of soft cow's-belly hide might just as well be gnawing toys.

Sue and Doug had led the procession to Farndale in their smart green pick-up, which serves a useful practical purpose as a mobile advertising hoarding for the East Riding Koi Co. Ltd. Not untypically of MMOC members, Sue is a one-type-of-Minor woman. Vans and pick-ups are her thing. 'My granddad had a van, and my Dad was a builder, so he had one too,' she says. 'Luckily Chris shares my taste, and we tracked this car down in Keighley in 2002, bought her and had her resprayed.' The Akrills enjoy company, and they joined an owner's club, but unfortunately it was troubled with the dissent and ill-feeling which often afflicts voluntary organisations. 'It was a battlefield,' says Sue bluntly. 'So we left and helped set up the Brid and Wolds instead.'

The pick-up is parked next to a beautiful dove grey saloon owned by Tom Dixon. Flitford Grey is the correct BMC term, although the narrow red stripe along the sides is all Dixon's own work ('My go-faster stripe,' he says). This is a Series 2 with four doors, a highly desirable Minor when it left the factory in 1959: powerful and easy to get passengers in and out of. Tom's first Minor was a much simpler model, bought in 1952, but it lasted long enough for his two sons to learn to drive in it. They liked the car, and a few years later one of them helped to revive the connection between the Dixon family and Morris Minors.

He's a biker, and he was out for a spin in the Dales one day when he saw a lovely cream Morris Traveller. He was due to get married and knew that his bride's family had owned a Traveller, so he stopped on the spur of the moment and asked if he could hire the car for his wedding day.

Yes, said the owner and it was all a huge success. Tom and his wife Jill were inspired by the romantic gesture to look for a Traveller of their own, homing in on one in Jarrow but finding to their disappointment that it suffered from the make's most common affliction, rotten wood. They carried on searching, found the 1959 four-door on a trip to the Midlands and settled for that instead.

Tom restored the car in 1998, using practical skills honed in his career as the engineer in charge of the *Yorkshire Post* building in Leeds. A Morris Minor was a doddle compared to this Brutalist lump of experimental architecture in which many peculiar things could, and did, go wrong. 'It was more a way of life than a job,' he says. Liz worked as a receptionist at Leeds United football club, in its heyday under Howard Wilkinson, and doesn't recall any Morris Minors in the players' car park. Premier League stars had grander tastes, much like the Dixons' two sons when they were at primary school.

They used to insist that we dropped them well away from the entrance if we were in the Moggy, so that none of their friends would see it. They told us it wasn't modern enough.

The car has most of its original features, including a steering wheel with delicate spokes and trafficator 'flickers' on the side struts, as well as the conventional flashing orange lights which the Dixons have added. 'I'd have stuck with just the semaphore,' says Tom, using yet another term for the little orange blade which springs up to signal a left or right turn. 'But these days, drivers don't notice them, so I thought we'd be safer having flashing lights as well.' The boot has the car's original bright red starting handle that doubles as a wheel brace for punctures: one of those simple, sturdy components which are at the heart of the Minor's appeal. A flat battery on a cold morning holds fewer terrors when you know you can crank the engine over like a Royal Flying Corps pilot with his biplane. There are always parts available too, says Tom. The only one that eluded him for ages was a new bonnet, but even these come on to the market from time to time, usually in curious ways. The Dixons stumbled on an example when they were on holiday in New Zealand. In a suburb of Christchurch they spotted a garage with the familiar Yorkshire name of Wakefield and in its yard a wavy sea of curving Morris Minor roofs.

There were sixty-five of them there, and the garage owner was closing down and selling up. A lot of the cars came back to the UK, and there was a sudden abundance of wings.

Tom was the first of a series of club members I met on the walk and over tea in the village hall who chimed exactly with Colin Buchanan's description of his own mechanical enthusiasm in *Mixed Blessing*. For all that he had become immensely eminent as a planner and traffic guru, there was nothing the Professor liked more than engaging in battle with a car's workings. He relished the prospect of long journeys in old cars because of the high chance of something going wrong and the prospect of trying to outwit the faulty ignition, timing or carburettor. He admitted that he would find it 'difficult to face life without an internal combustion engine of some kind to pit my wits against' and regretted – accurately – that a time would come when cars' engines were sealed and packaged and as 'taboo to the amateur as the inside of a television set.' In the year he wrote the book, 1957, a car had appeared for the first time without a starting handle, which he considered the beginning of the end. But that was to overlook the staying power of the Morris Minor. There are starting handles to spare at Farndale.

Graham and Jacqueline Steenhoven from Hutton Cranswick have parked their 1968 saloon alongside, a car made close to the end of Morris Minor production but subsequently modernised much more. It has an original metal sun visor sticking out above the windscreen like the peak of a soldier's helmet, but the comfy front seats with their headrests are cannibalised from a Metro, as is the 1300cc engine, which gives the car the oomph for motorways.

> She does 40 mpg and flies up hills. The only one she failed was near Goathland, a couple of valleys away from here across the moors, where the slope was 30 per cent (one in three).

The car crawled to a halt and the Steenhovens had to drive out in reverse. But that was a rare failure, and the couple use the Morris as their everyday car in summer, when its relatively spartan interior lets in less in the way of rain and chill. Graham is a gardener and Jackie a senior carer, and the economies of Minor motoring are significant. As Graham says:

It's much cheaper to run than our other car, a Volvo 440. There's no tax, because it's a classic car, and we pay £80 for fully comprehensive insurance. The only iffy thing's the MOT, but we've just been through that.

Graham brings a sentimental heritage to his Minor. His Dutch father drove an ex-Army Traveller, rather than one of the vans or pick-ups which the Morris offshoot in Holland specialised in making. He taught his son about how Britain's class structure in the 1950s was reflected in military Travellers. The Minor had a deserved reputation as a car which appealed to everyone and came within a wide range of budgets, but the Army still found a way of making nice distinctions. Officers had four door models, like the Steenhovens'. Other ranks got two doors. But family feeling is diluting in spite of LFJ 230F's smart Trafalgar Blue livery, peppy engine and comfy front seats. Jackie admits: 'I find it a bit annoying when I can't get all my shopping in, and the kids aren't so keen.' All of them are teenagers −13, 15 and 17 − and they don't like being dropped off near school any more than Tom and Liz Dixon's sons did. They also usually have to sit on the back seat, which is the Minor's original one, bench-style and nowhere near as comfy as the Metro inserts in front. When Graham bought the car in Bristol, where Charlie Ware handled the restoration, he discovered that its previous owner had had a similar one stolen. 'It's quite a problem down south, especially with restored cars,' he says – although the Steenhoven teens may take some convincing of that.

Sheena and Paul Botterill's Minor brings a cheerier slant on the next generation's likely attitude to the ageing car. It's bulging with the couple's grandchildren, who swap turns at the wheel in the car park, pretending to drive, and tell me that they love Maurice – the family's name for the 1969 saloon – 'because it takes us to the seaside'. Like H.E. Bates's Larkin family, more and more people seem to spill out of the car, as Sheena manoeuvres cheerfully and nearly reverses into Penny as she photographs another car. 'Sheena's the one most likely to run you over,' confides Sue Akrill, loud enough for her friend to hear, but Sheena doesn't mind a bit. She launches into telling me how she once drove off with the boot open, and how her brother Graham used to race old Ford Anglias and got so famous that Corgi made a children's model of one of his cars. Paul, a big, beaming joiner who's defied a soaking to escort the Daffodil rally in his beach buggy, is the club's king of panel-making. He bought sheets of eight- by four-feet steel from a metal fabricator on Driffield industrial estate and himself has hammered out most of a new set of bodywork panels for Maurice. Graham has come along too, in his retro Chrysler, and Paul says: 'Come over and look at its front doors. Aren't they incredibly like a Morris Minor's?' They are, both in overall shape and the curving sill at the base. Maurice is another Minor that has benefited from family sentiment. Sheena had always wanted one because she grew up with her father's and saw how fond he was of it. Paul took the hint and master-minded a restoration – from Maurice's sad old MOT failure state – which saw most of the car remade as new. 'If summat's to be done,' he says, in a motto very appropriate to the sturdy Minor tradition, 'I want it done a hundred and fifty per cent.'

More engineers appear. While about half of the rally teams have marched off along the Dove to see the daffodils – beautiful descendants of plants which were probably introduced to Yorkshire by French monks – Norman Metcalfe and Richard Hall are comfortably set up with tea and cakes, provided by Farndale Women's Institute in the village hall. I'm already impressed by the level of knowledge concentrated in this very small sample of Minor expertise, but Metcalfe and Hall take it a stage further. Retired now, Norman was Chief Operations Inspector on the Humber Bridge, looking after this wonderful example of design and engineering between 1981 and 2003. He is one of a handful of people who have walked the entire length of a mile and a third *inside* the concrete roadway compartments, stepping into each narrow, hollow space through a small hatch in the connecting wall. The hidden route is sealed up now to keep out moisture, so few people, if any, will experience such a techie's treat again. In between times, Norman has owned thirty-nine cars, starting and ending (for now) with Morris Minors. His current one is very special; one of Issigonis's original 'low lights' (with the headlamps incorporated into the radiator grille), which the designer so much preferred to the later and better-known adaptation with the lights in the wings. 'I like its reliability and the fact that people look at it,' he says. 'I owned two others in between. I've always been fond of the Minor, because it was my first car and I wanted to stay with it. I got to feel almost a part of it, like a centaur.' His wife Jean likes the car too, and the couple call it Chester (with Field as its rarely used surname, because they bought it in Chesterfield). Jean, who worked in a solicitor's office in Hull before she retired, isn't quite such an enthusiast but she is certainly a valued part of the Metcalfe motoring team. 'She is a brilliant pillion rider,' says Norman, with warmth. They both enjoy two wheels as well as four.

Richard Hall, supping his tea across the trestle table from the Metcalfes, also spent his working life immersed in complex and brilliant design and technology. For most of the thirty-eight years he has owned his 1956 split-screen Minor he worked for British Aerospace at Brough on the Humber estuary. He was a production engineer on aircraft such as the Royal Navy's *Buccaneer*, the *Trident* passenger jet and the *Hawk* trainer. He became a specialist in computer work but retained a feel for hands-on work, which explains why his Minor corners as well as a Mini Cooper. As well as a more powerful engine and smoother gearbox, he has installed telescopic suspension. The result is a classic modern Minor; traditional on the outside but with plenty of beef in the mechanical works. Hall, who is fifty-seven, bought the car in 1970 from a fellow apprentice at Brough, a schoolfriend who had had the car for a year, so Richard could see that it wasn't rubbish. He used it happily for years as a cheap runabout until the brakes and suspension got tatty, so he drove it into a farm shed and retirement in mothballs. But the need to get his hands on some well-designed machinery in need of affection was too strong, and in 2001 he dragged the car back into the daylight and spent three years restoring it. The work was done to very high standards, down to the famous four-inch section in the bumpers where Alec Issigonis had chopped his initial design in half.

There was a wonderful Minor expert in Hessle called Kevin Brown, who really loved these cars. I helped him out for a couple of years in his workshop and learned a lot. You'll find restorers who ask what you want and do it, but Kevin wasn't like that. He'd say: 'Yes, I can do it, but what you really want to do with your car is this . . . or that.' He wanted them perfect, rather than just repairing them.

Hall is in the same mould. As well as two Travellers, his personal fleet of Minors includes a saloon as a source of parts and panels. 'I've tried some of the newly-made panels and they don't always fit properly,' he says. 'In fact some of them look more like bits of a Ford Anglia.'

Penny, meanwhile, is reliving old student-days nightmares involving the butterfly nuts on her convertible's roof with Tim Stanforth, a fifty-year-old mechanic from Driffield who has even worse tales to tell. He and his wife Pam ('Is she interested? I'd have to say more that she suffers') have two convertibles and plenty of experience of their quirks. 'One time the roof whipped off when I was doing 60 mph; it just held on by one of the struts,' says Tim. 'Oh, and I don't like those butterfly nuts. The roof comes off easily enough, but it can be a business getting it up and secured.' The Stanforths bought their second convertible from a man in the pub car park in Sledmere who came over to look at their Minor and said: 'I've got one like that in a shed at home.' Tim couldn't bear the thought of a captive, neglected convertible and his kindness was repaid. Poking about underneath the car, he found the letters MAT on the chassis, which mean a genuine factory convertible; many of the others on the road, including Tim and Pam's other car, were originally saloons whose roofs were sliced off and sides strengthened. There's more of that family heritage in the Stanforth cars, too. Tim's father had a bottle green Minor which worked its charms on the family.

But now there were cheery shouts from outside, and Sue came marching back after getting as far up the daffodil valley as everyone could manage without wellies. There was hustle and bustle and cries of 'Don't be late or we'll miss our lunch', and everyone shambled out and headed for the line of Minors like RAF pilots scrambling for a Battle of Britain sortie. Sue came over to say goodbye and answer my last question: Why do we like the Morris Minor so much? It was lent force by all the weekend walkers clustering round the cars, from greybeards who knew them well to children who just liked their smiling radiators and coy, lidded headlights. 'Well,' she said, 'everyone loves a poached egg on wheels, don't they? They smile too – don't they look happy, those little cars over there?' They did; and better was to come. Growl, pop, harrrum . . . nothing beats the sound of a row of Morris Minors starting up: year after year of Minor memories came back as the poached eggs swung out of the car park and along the lane, a line of friendly little shapes getting smaller and smaller as they wound up the moorland road to have lunch and swap more stories at the Lion Inn on Blakey Ridge.

It was great to spend time with a bunch of enthusiasts, all of them new to me. But I wondered what it was like to live day after day with a companion devoted to a Morris Minor, and I knew just the person to tell me. Lillian McPhee has been a friend since I kidnapped her late husband Don on an almost daily basis to come with me on *Guardian* assignments around the North of England. He was a kind and thoughtful man who, like me, placed considerable importance on breaking our work to have lunch, and as a result we had many excellent chats. I soon discovered that he was a Minor man and over the years I enjoyed pictures of his convertible at home in the Cheshire village of Poynton, in the wilds of Ireland and with a convoy of thirty other Moggies exploring forgotten corners of France.

Don was a photojournalist of the first rank, a veteran of

Northern Ireland, where he was car-jacked at gunpoint, and United States presidential campaigns, where he developed film by torchlight in a motel bathroom's basin before bluffing his way on to Air Force One. But he was also a very cosy man, with a devoted family and exactly the interests you would expect of a Morris Minor enthusiast. He owned a canal barge, which he skippered with a jaunty peaked cap, and he sedulously followed *Coronation Street*. His younger daughter Ailsa, a primary school teacher who shares her father's energy and dedication, recalls a magic moment in her pre-teens:

> I was meant to be doing my homework but we were watching Corrie instead, when guess what drove into the Street? 'Dad! Dad! They've got a Morris Minor on Corrie!' I can hear it now and see his face.

Her mother Lil is a gutsy woman, born Lillian LaRose to a father who served on a Belgian submarine in the war and was thankfully on leave when it sank. Lil's own mother is from Manchester, daughter of Honest Alf Herd, a bookmaker and one of the founding members of the Bookmaker's Protection Association (which protected the public, rather than bookies, by trying to keep rogues out of the trade). Lil is certainly not someone to take second place to a mere car. But she was responsible for Don's love affair with a Minor; soon after they had got married, he realised that her life would be a great deal easier with a runabout. A Morris Traveller appeared.

'Don didn't have a thing about Morris Minors at that stage. It could have been any cheap and easy car,' she says. 'But when our friends saw the car, they all said: "You want to talk to Alf in the village if anything goes wrong and needs sorting out."' Alf was a member of the British Morris Minor Owners' Club, and Don soon got interested. As with cameras, his canal barge, and even the furniture in the *Guardian's* Manchester office, he was interested in anything technical and the way it worked. He was a perfectionist as well as an enthusiast, and once he had decided to do something, he would do it to the highest standards. He was soon a lively member of the MMOC, attending local meetings, sending photographs to the club's magazine *Minor Matters* (quite something, any professional photographer will tell you, to have Don McPhee working for you free) and taking daytrips in search of spares to places such as Charlie Ware's centre in Bath. The Traveller was joined by the classy convertible, and Lil lost ninety per cent of her odd-jobs space in the family's garage.

Once again, though, she was an accessory to the deed. Don had agreed that the Traveller was getting a bit too unpredictable and accepted Lil's plans to buy a second-hand Renault 4 'pig wagon', an upmarket relative to the doughty Citroen 2CV on French farms.

Then we were browsing through the papers, and Don saw an advert for the convertible. We went to see it, and the woman who owned it was asking rather a lot. Don said 'I'm not paying that,' and we were set to walk away. But I told him: 'You know, Don, if you don't buy her, you'll always regret it.' The deal was done.

The Minor moved into the garage and was soon lovingly swaddled in blankets. Don consulted the barometer every time he and Lil took her out, and kept the keys hidden from the rest of the family. I don't think Lil ever told him, but she admitted to me that her older daughter Lizzie and her boyfriend discovered the spare keys and once, just once, secretly took the precious car for a spin. Thank goodness, they didn't hit anything or scrape a hedge, and the few flicks of mud and dust were covertly wiped off.

It was like a shrine. When we had workmen in the house, they'd hear about the Minor, and I'd go in and they'd be there with Don and the bonnet raised, all going 'Mmmm' and 'Aaaah'. Meanwhile, I used to have trouble getting to my washing machine and finding somewhere to put spare stuff, and I'd ring Don and say things like 'I'm going to break every window in that car.'

But he knew she didn't mean it, and in his soft Manchester voice he'd always say the same thing: 'It isn't doing any harm.'

Lil, Ailsa and Lizzie drew the line at joining Don's grommet-hunting expeditions to Bath or similar techno-outings, but they all sailed happily off in the Minor for picnics, club treasure hunts and open-top tours through the glories of the Peak District and the Pennines. Don and Lil had some memorable crossings to Ireland for the annual Morris Minor festival in Bandon, near Cork. 'You should have seen it,' says Lil, brandishing a wooden love-spoon entwined with the Irish tricolour which she and Don won in one of the festival's many mad events. 'An entire village cut off, with every car in sight a Morris Minor, and the local priest going round carefully blessing them all.'

This was a rehearsal for a series of much longer breaks which became part of the McPhee family's summer calendar: MoT – not the test that every Minor has to face every year, but Minors on Tour. If you look out a copy of *Minor Matters* for July/August 1992, you'll see a typically fine Don McPhee colour photograph on the cover – the convertible creeping through the half-timbered Alsace town of Ribeauvillé, with Lil looking more than slightly anxious at the wheel while Ailsa stands in the front passenger seat with her hair flung back and wielding a big straw hat to salute passers-by. 'Heard of Ribeauvillé? Neither had I,' says Lil,

> and that was the wonderful thing about MoT. They took us all over France to places where most tourists never go. We discovered hidden bits of Brittany and the Loire and, best of all, Ribeauvillé. They've got so many storks there, it's incredible.

The back cover of the same issue has another McPhee photograph, of a stork stalking past a green Traveller. If it inspected all the MoT participants, it would have seen almost a hundred cars, from Germany, Switzerland, the Netherlands and Scandinavia as well as the UK. Among them there was also a Minor belonging to a Frenchman from the next village, who knew nothing about the rally but suddenly encountered a line of more Morris Minors than he had ever seen in his life and joined the end to find out what was going on. I know how he felt. One of the best pictures Don ever showed me was of an MoT convoy snaking through the French countryside, a vast version of the Yorkshire procession tootling up from Farndale to Blakey Ridge.

The French joined in the swing of things, says Lil. They were pleased to see English people behaving eccentrically, and, for the men in particular, the common bond of gaskets and distributors transcends all national boundaries. A club is a club, however, and even the report in *Minor Matters* by Mary Hall refers to a member, after a welcome banquet, observing: 'It's a bit French, this meal.' It wasn't Don, but Lil recalls how she had to badger him to experiment with French cuisine and – conscious of her own half-Walloon ancestry – try out his schoolboy French. He suffered, like many of us, from the agonies of screwing up delicate French pronunciation in the manner of Sir Winston Churchill and Ted Heath, but one evening, when Lil had stayed in their tent at the campsite because she was feeling ill, he came back bright-eyed from the local brasserie.

'You'd have loved it, Lil,' he said. 'We had your favourite, *moules marinière*, and they were all very sympathetic when they asked why I was alone and I told them about you.'

'Ah, darling, what did you say?' she asked.

'I said "Ma femme est merde",' replied Don proudly, unaware that he had muddled the French for 'shit' with 'malade' meaning 'ill'.

It sounds like a shaggy dog story, but Lil doesn't tell fibs, and anyway I can see all the Frenchmen gathered round Don, nodding in misconceived sympathy at his need to get away from the wife.

Mary Hall's article about her own ten years' experience of MoT chimes with what I know of Don and what I saw at Farndale, so far as the bonds that link Morris Minor enthusiasts are concerned. The foreign jaunts

> epitomise all that is best about owning and driving Minors and belonging to the MMOC. The emphasis is on using the cars, not showing off their shiny bits. . . . There aren't any concours prizes, so the one thing nobody takes is polish, and anyone seen washing their Minor is likely to get fined. . . . The MoTs are also about people. The camaraderie is something special.

Members have watched babies grow into teenagers and friendships into marriages. All human life is there, says Mary.

Mind you, there is plenty of prize-hunting in the wider world of Minor clubbing. The McPhees had a cupboard full of plaques for best-polished convertible and the like, which Lil passed on to the friend – it had to be a friend – who bought the car after Don's death from cancer in March 2007. The summer fasti of rallies and meets involves line after line, in field after park, of immaculate Minors, proud restorations and arcane rarities, especially in specialist realms such as commercial vehicles or customisations. It's not unpleasant, either, to have the chance of meeting celebrity owners of the car: famous Minoristas such as Bryan Ferry, Lord Linley, Stirling Moss and one of the Royal chauffeurs at Buckingham Palace. And the car has an extraordinary place in British culture, of every sort; even, as I was about to discover, when rusting in a farmyard with chickens inside and a blackbird nesting in the boot.

Chapter 7
Minor Monuments

*If broomsticks were cars, this one would be a split-window
Morris Minor.*

Terry Pratchett, *Equal Rites*, 1987

 IN 1980 THE IRISH HEALTH authorities
decided to employ a new speech therapist in
County Leitrim, a decision that was to have
unexpected consequences for the cultural
history of the Morris Minor. The job went
to a young applicant from Hebden Bridge in West
Yorkshire, Susie Mitchell, whose partner Martin Parr was a
photographer recording life in Calderdale with the help of
a grant from the Arts Council. The couple took two steps to
prepare for their new life on the west coast of Ireland: they
got married, because the Celtic tiger had not yet bitten the
heels of the all-powerful Catholic church, and they bought a
classic Morris Minor.

The car was a split-screen model whose date of manufacture, according to its previous owner, was either 1952 or
1953 – an imprecision that suited the Parrs because Martin
was born in 1952 and Susie a year later. They lovingly
restored it but never completely conquered various glitches

in its workings. By the time they drove on to the Irish Sea ferry, they were already well-accustomed to a constant search for spares, even though the old car was gleaming without and spick-and-span within, and admired by all who saw it.

In such circumstances a Morris Minor owner develops a sort of sixth sense which spots a familiar curve or radiator grille in the most unlikely situations. As Martin and Susie drove across Ireland to their new home in Sligo, they realised that this sense was working overtime. The further west they went, the more abandoned Morris Minors they discovered, in fields, in hencoops, peeping out of barns and even in the sea, where their barnacled shapes emerged at low tide. 'We'd be driving along, and one or other of us would shout "There's one!," and we'd screech to a halt,' says Martin. Initially, the aim was to hunt for a sprocket or a wheel nut for their own recalcitrant car, but he quickly developed another purpose.

The lost cars were a photographer's dream, each seeming to have its own poignant setting, peculiar new use and hints for the imagination to construct a life story. There was a lovely old convertible tilting into a duck pond on the Dingle peninsular, a drenched saloon under sheets of rain in the emptiest part of Connemara. To his delight, Martin found a thrush's nest under the gaping bonnet of a Minor at Toomard, and a specially fine sea wreck – he mentally classified these as 'Coastal Morris Minors' – fifty yards off the beach at Ashheaton in County Limerick. Was it driven spectacularly into the waves, or quietly pushed at night? He did not find out, but the car made a marvellous photograph. Bumper to bumper, it was entirely covered in seaweed.

Rapidly, the portfolio grew, and, although Parr was busy photographing many other sides of Ireland, the Morris Minor collection took on a life of its own. At the Galway Festival in 1982 it made the leap from a private hobby to a public exhibition: more than forty photos were displayed in a show called *Abandoned Morris Minors of the West of Ireland*. By chance, I was in Hebden Bridge at the time and screeched to my own halt (in a Vauxhall Astra by then, not a Morris Minor) when I saw in a window a poster with this arresting title. Alas, the poster of the poster was an old friend of the Parrs loyally doing his bit for the faraway exhibition in Ireland, and the pictures were not to be seen in Hebden Bridge. But the phrase has stuck in my mind.

After Galway, Parr continued work on a larger collection, eventually published as a book entitled *A Fair Day*, which brought together the woebegone Morris Minors with four other aspects of Irish life, from ballroom dancing to bungalows. It was a prestigious project that needed a catalogue, and Parr had noticed the work of a young journalist on the *Irish Times* called Fintan O'Toole. 'You can spot a good writer,' he says, 'and Fintan was at the beginning of what has become an illustrious career.' (Now a prominent writer, historian and literary critic in Ireland, Fintan O'Toole had also embarked on a scrutiny of Irish politics, which has made him one of the best-known scourges of the Dail's repeated problems with corruption.)

In his Georgian house on the steep slopes between Clifton and the Avon Gorge in Bristol – a sort of upmarket Hebden Bridge of the South-West – Martin has a unique souvenir of the project: a copy of *A Fair Day* signed by both O'Toole, who accepted Parr's commission to write the text, and Charles Haughey, then the Taoiseach, who opened the exhibition but had clashed with O'Toole repeatedly in print. 'With best wishes to the artist from Charles Haughey,' says the scribble from the Taoiseach. 'Adios partner. Fintan,' O'Toole has written underneath.

Parr finds it significant that the only one of the five sections for which O'Toole thought that words were unnecessary was the Morris Minor one. Lost, abandoned, semi-submerged, the sadness of the pictures, in Fintan's opinion, needed no text. The nearest he came to the subject was in another chapter, where he lingered briefly on the extraordinary story of the Shamrock, the brainchild of Tennessee expatriate William T. Curtis, who in 1959 built a factory in Tralee, County Kerry, to mass-produce an all-Irish version of the big-finned saloons that dominated the American car market at the time. A cross between a 1957 Thunderbird and a Studebaker Hawk in appearance, the fibreglass monster would have been madness on Ireland's twisting country roads, and it also suffered from a hopelessly underpowered Austin A55 engine. Mending a puncture in a rear wheel involved unbolting the entire axle, and mass production stopped altogether after only eight cars. The factory had moved in the middle of the process to Castleblayney, County Monaghan, where the only surviving

Shamrock in working order (maintained by its owner Paddy Byrne in Drogheda, County Louth) makes regular appearances at the town's annual show. In keeping with the mournful atmosphere of Parr's abandoned Morris Minors, the whole of the rest of the Shamrock enterprise – unused parts, fibreglass body shells and machine tools – was dumped in Lake Muckno on the edge of the town.

The book made Parr a national figure in Ireland, and his letterbox regularly received tips about other picturesquely rotting cars, often addressed just to 'Martin Parr, Morris Minor Collector' or 'The Morris Minor Man, Boyle, Ireland'. 'They would ask "Do you know about this sighting and that relic, almost gone now but just worth catching?"' he says, and off he went in pursuit.

There were Minors covered in birds' nests, converted into hen houses, sheltering ducks by a pond near Dingle, and there was always plenty of great craic if you met anyone nearby. Not that you did, much. That was part of the surreal nature of the exercise. You'd get out, take the photographs and occasionally someone would drift up, but mostly the Morris Minors were on their own. I photographed the occasional abandoned Beetle and once or twice a Citroen 2CV, but the Minor was always the thing. The shape was pleasing. It worked. It had a symmetry. It stayed until you were down to the last six inches of car – even with a little relic like that, the wreckage still came through as a Morris Minor. It never lost its glory for a moment, even when almost everything had disappeared. It was all marvellous,

except for this: the one thing Susie and I never did get out of
the project was a single spare part for our own car.

Before I left Martin's house to catch the train from
Temple Meads to Oxford and the Lord Nuffield social club,
he showed me a beautiful little silver brooch with an
unmistakable shape. It was a Morris Minor front door, and
I could get one, said Martin, if I contacted a friend of his in
the village of Ugford near Salisbury. Soon afterwards I was
hearing the story of the door direct from its maker John
Barker, who was a student of jewellery and silversmithing in
the wood, metal and ceramics department at Manchester
Polytechnic when Parr was studying photography there.
Barker's parents were both in arts education, and he had
considered the idea of becoming a teacher himself, but
silversmithing turned out to offer him an instant living. He
made pieces at college during the day and sold them in the
pub at night, while at the same time developing a serious
reputation with gallery exhibitions.

Like so many of us in his generation in the 1960s and
1970s, Barker went through a series of Morris Minors,
along with other cars. He was never a Moggies-only man.
But he liked them because they were practical, as he was.
'Reliable, affordable, cheap to run, instantly lucrative and
for ever practical,' he says. He lit on the door as what he
called 'the distillation of the car.' He had made a number of
one-off car-part pieces, some on commission from people
who wanted a scrap of miniature Bentley or whatever, and
he also went through a series of damaged mini-parts: a bent

bumper which made what he considered a pleasingly organic shape; a battered Rolls Royce radiator grille which he supposes now was a political statement at the tail end of student revolt. The door was something else. Almost, in today's cliché, an icon. 'It is instantly recognisable, essential visually to the Minor, unmistakable,' he says. The market certainly thought so too. By 1975 he was selling hundreds of the brooches, and demand lasted well into the 1980s. They were cast from a mould, but each one needed a fair amount of careful finishing off. In recent years he has moved from jewellery to sculpture and other projects, but he still casts a few Minor doors on a regular basis:

> I doubt today's young woman would consciously want a Morris Minor car door, but the shape seems to have a wider resonance. There have always been plenty of people who bought one and didn't know what it was. They just liked the shape. That's part of the brilliance of the car's design, surely.

Last year, though no Minor fanatic, Barker found himself buying two ancient split-screen models.

> I'd driven a Citroen 2CV for ten years and something inside me said: try a Minor again. It was a shock getting into such an old car, with things such as windscreen wipers which seemed to do one wipe every fifteen seconds. I suppose at my age – 57 – I should be getting an enormous motorbike as part of that going back to your youth thing. But in my case

it's expressed itself through owning a Minor again, for the first time in twenty-five years.

He loves it, even though the one of the two which is roadworthy is arthritic and has him wondering if it will make it, even when he drives the simple mile into Wilton and back to get provisions. He's also still casting the doors. You can order one from The Old Farm in Ugford for £35. I got one for Penny to mark our 2008 wedding anniversary and to apologise – in a way – for talking rather a lot about the Morris Minor between January and June.

Some years after Martin Parr's exhibition, my colleague Don McPhee compiled a similar dossier, not under Parr's influence but coming fresh to the same forlorn subjects while criss-crossing Ireland with writer David Ward to illustrate *Guardian* stories about the Irish drift-net salmon fishery and the pilgrims' airport being built, to much incredulity, in bogland near the remote Catholic shrine of Knock. I have already described Don's enthusiasm for Moggies, but not the high point in this side of his life. It came when the hugely successful Commonwealth Games at Manchester in 2002 ended with a cavalcade of the bulbous little cars. It was raining, there were tight deadlines, and the closing ceremony had many other attractions, but Don's face was a picture – lit up as if by one of his own flashbulbs. He clicked away as the forty-one cars formed the centre of a Busby Berkeley dance routine in front of the Queen and Prime Minister Tony Blair, before disgorging the celebrated couple Ashley and Maxine from *Coronation Street* and a troupe of Viennese waltzers. His marvellous pictures appeared in the *Guardian*, but the next day they also appeared in the email box of Rosemary Hamilton of the Morris Minor Owners' Club, which had not been able to hire its own photographer because of short notice and the secrecy of the event. After Don's untimely death from cancer in 2007, Rosemary wrote to the newspaper to describe how he had ''phoned his wife to let her know he would be late and to ask her to video the broadcast of the ceremony [she later told me he was so excited, he was like a little boy at Christmas]. He then settled down to take the beautiful photographs that we will treasure.'

These were posted on the MMOC website along with Rosemary's description of the ingenious ballet, which saw club member Sandy Hamilton drive his Trafalgar Blue Minor into the stadium at the head of the procession. On board with him was the *Coronation Street* posse, with Tracey Shaw, who plays Maxine, bubbling, 'My Dad had a car just like this one.' Teachers, a nurse, a solicitor, a prison officer and a hospital consultant were among the other drivers who painstakingly took the cars through a series of choreographed manoeuvres before forming a neat square in the centre of the ring. Applause was tumultuous as the sequence happily overran its original eight minutes to last for quarter of an hour.

Don recorded many mass outings of Morris Minors for the *Guardian* and *Minor Matters* alike, returning to Ireland several times and compiling an excellent portfolio of the goings-on in the Morris-Minor-only streets of Bandon in 2003. It was an inspiring sight, and one which, along with Martin Parr's photographs, may have inspired another. In the Dublin suburb of Fingal at the time, young landscape gardener Peter Donegan was earning a name for imaginative twists on the usual offer of border shrubs, rockeries and decking. He had grown his first plants under his bed at the age of seven – geraniums and cacti – and his business did eye-catching things, such as heating its office by burning briquettes of old paperwork and posting the world's first garden-centre website written in Gaelic. In 2007 they hit the jackpot at the first *Bloom* exhibition in Phoenix Park with a silver medal for a garden with an unusual centrepiece: two-thirds of an abandoned Morris Minor. According to Donegan, it was designed 'to commemorate the many Irish men with initially great intentions, who promise to restore and rebuild projects but sometimes never fully complete them'. In a twist on the range of curious customising inflicted on Morris Minors, the shell was fitted with com-fortable seats and video and audio equipment 'to become an entertainment area of sorts, which should give the feeling that, even if forgotten, the life of the garden continued to flourish around it'.

It may be coincidence, but the designer David Linley – strictly speaking, Lord Linley, the Queen's nephew and eleventh in line to the throne – has also made cars the centrepieces of small gardens, including one at a show. At his second home in France, he created a garden to com-plement his Citroen 2CV, with terraced beds surrounding the area where the car is parked. In 2003 he expanded on the idea with a garden surrounding a Citroen C3 at the *Daily Telegraph* House and Garden fair in Olympia. 'I'm trying to evoke a Provençal spirit with it,' he said at the time. 'It's supposed to look as though there's a party going on. The car's doors are open, there's music playing, and it has a very French feel.' He has yet to feature a Morris Minor, although he owns the beautifully restored one which Joanna Wood told me about back in Hungerford in February. It can only be a matter of time.

Garden enthusiasts who sat in the Dublin *Bloom* car watching film clips on its TV are bound to have seen other Morris Minors on the screen. Issigonis's creation appeared in films almost as soon as it made its debut on the market. Many of the cars were simply part of the backdrop, especially in films from Ealing and other British studios, but Minors seemed to have an appeal to the much more sophisticated film-makers of the Continent and the big-money studios of Hollywood. The Swedes, who were about to embark on the glorious Bergman era, were particularly keen on Minors as prominent extras. In 1954 a split-screen model played a bit part in *Asa-Nisse pa hals is*, a movie that was primarily a vehicle for a Swedish favourite of the time: Bertil Boo, the Singing Farmer. A year earlier, one of the earliest Minors drove proudly through *Niagara*, a murder thriller starring Marilyn Monroe and promoted as 'A raging torrent of emotion that even Nature can't control'. Most viewers tended to focus on the mayhem or Monroe, but not Minor enthusiasts. They were intrigued that the car was the 'low light' type, which was barred from the United States on safety grounds. The answer was that this one came from Canada, which shares the Niagara Falls with the States, and was allowed into the US as a visitor.

French cinema went for a Minor in 1955 in *Les Diaboliques*, a masterly suspense film, again in *Les Suspects* in 1957, more thrills in colonial Algeria, and also in Eric Rohmer's 1959 comedy *La Signe du Lion*. All three were convertibles, which are the nearest a Morris Minor can hope to approach to the élan of chic French style. Another 'ragtop', as aficionados call the convertibles, was used by the Italian master Michelangelo Antonioni in his early satire on the world of film-makers, *La Signora senza Camelie* in 1953. Taken together, the cinema playbills for the car would fill the walls of Britain's biggest Odeon several times, and they include plenty of both cinema classics and blockbusters. Jean-Luc Godard's *Une Femme est une Femme* has a Minor, and so does *The Day of the Jackal*. The master of such macho cars as the Aston Martin DB5 with added machine guns and ejector seat, James Bond, is driven to his hotel in a Morris Minor in *Thunderball* (inevitably, a convertible). Both the Beatles' films *A Hard Day's Night* and *Help!* feature Morris Minors, and the Cliff Richard vehicle *The Young Ones* has one too, although the film devotes far more footage to that other great icon of modern British road transport, the London Routemaster bus.

The Minor's greatest moments in film may well lie just ahead, however, judging by the track record of the much-fêted and -Oscared director Peter Jackson. Garlanded with awards for his *Lord of the Rings* trilogy, he had an unusual relationship with Minors during his film-making apprentice-ship, possibly because he comes from one of their principal strongholds outside the United Kingdom, New Zealand. In his very early and very low-budget movie *Bad Taste* – made with a few pals and a single hand-held 16mm camera but later shown at the Cannes Film Festival – his hero only just escapes in his Morris Minor from the clutches of a hideous alien; the creature rips off the rear bumper. This was added to the script, according to cast members, after the real-life bumper of the car came off when its owner, the wife of the film's co-star Craig Smith, was moving house and hauling a seriously overloaded trailer. Watch the film carefully, and you may spot that the bumper, pre-alien encounter, is held on with a piece of string.

It was Jackson's next film which created perhaps the greatest cinematic moment for the Minor to date. A mad subversion of the celebrated Muppet puppets of Jim Henson, *Meet The Feebles* transformed the world of Kermit and Miss Piggy into a nightmare where cosy icons showed their sinister side. Cue the Minor, or rather an entire town full of them and no other cars, like Bandon during the Minor meet in Ireland. The film's horrible villain, a character called Bletch, drives a one-off black Minor stretch limousine with the registration BLETCH 1, whose whereabouts remain as much a mystery as the fate of the last, last, one-off Minor – supposedly made at Cowley in Oxford for a vicar. Needless to say, there is some crossover between Minor enthusiasts and devotees of Tolkien, and many hours have been spent vainly pausing DVDs of the three *Lord of the Rings* films to see if a Minor has been slipped in somewhere among the hobbits and orcs.

On television, the car has made as regular an appearance as those character actors whose talents cannot disguise the fact that, yes, it's dear, familiar old them again. A Trafalgar Blue convertible called Miriam was a mainstay of *Lovejoy*, the series based on the escapades of a roguish antique dealer, which seemed apposite to the car. A Minor was an obvious companion, too, for the clumsy but endearing Michael Crawford in *Some Mothers Do 'Ave 'Em*, especially in a cheeky end-of-episode nod to *The Italian Job*, which had filled cinemas five years earlier. Crawford hangs on to the rear bumper of his pale blue saloon as it teeters on a cliff edge. Luckily, a coachload of rugby players . . . but no, I mustn't spoil the suspense, in case you missed the episode ('Cliffhanger', screened November 1973) and want to hire a DVD. You can also buy the official model of this accident-prone car for £16.95 in the Corgi Classics series.

Lynda Baron as Nurse Gladys Emmanuel naturally drove a Minor in *Open All Hours*, allowing Ronnie Barker, as her tireless suitor Albert Arkwright, to make comparisons between her curves and the car's. She was pink and the Minor was ivory, but otherwise there was a resemblance, and the series writer Roy Clarke seems to have known the car's hazards. He didn't go so far as to have a bonnet fly off, as happened to me and at Sir Alec Issigonis's Alvis trial, but in one episode Arkwright's trousers became detached from the Minor and wrapped themselves round the face of a following motor cyclist. And then there was *George and Mildred*, with the argumentative pair scooting round in a Snowberry White convertible with red trimming and the hugely valuable numberplate TEL 999. 'She's still trying to steer him to romance. He doesn't know what she's driving at,' said the playbills, reinforcing the image of a car that was lovable but not a babe-magnet. In *Red Dwarf* Rimmer is challenged to produce his dream car and, in the batty style of the series, lurches first to a Reliant Robin and then the other way to an E-type Jaguar; finally, a Morris Minor emerges and proves lasting: the perfect, popular compromise.

Musically, the Minor has also made its mark, even if we have yet to see some talented wag come up with a Symphony in A Minor. But who can overlook Morris Minor and the Majors, whose single *Stutter Rap (No Sleep 'til Bedtime)* reached number four in the UK singles chart in 1988, on the back of the Beastie Boys, the American hip-hop group who were very big news at the time. MM&TM was the idea of Tony Hawks, a young musician who toured the pubs and wine bars of London in the evening, playing the piano and singing for peanuts to pay for his daytime obsession with writing one of the world's great songs. He was good: he reached the final of the Vivien Ellis Prize for Young Composers for the Musical Stage. But it was only when he abandoned the serious genre and turned to comedy that he made his modest breakthrough.

Now a successful author of books such as *Round Ireland*

with a Fridge, he looks back on the MM&TM days fondly, but gives the credit to his father. Hawks was looking for song ideas, and his dad thought of English icons and said: 'What about the Morris Minor?' Tony thought: Yes, wrote a hymn to the car and entered it for a TV talent contest called *The Fame Game*. They invited him to perform it on air, which meant sorting out a group at high speed from his many musical friends and finding a name for it even more quickly. Morris Minor and the Majors was the choice, and it stuck when record producers offered a contract after the TV appearance. They were a one-hit wonder, although quite an impressive one; the single sold 220,000 copies worldwide and actually topped the charts in Australia. Its follow-up, *This Is the Chorus*, appealed to the Aussies to some extent, reaching number 22, but in the UK it stopped at 95.

Tony wrote and starred in a short-lived TV series, *Morris Minor's Marvellous Motors*, which featured a bandleader trying to combine his singing career with running a garage. Viewers never found out what happened in the end, though, as it never got a second series. Hawks went on to make his name in other fields, while fighting a cheerful but losing battle with people who confuse him with the American skateboarding champion Tony Hawk. 'Each week,' he says on his website, 'I receive email from young people all over the world congratulating me on my skateboarding prowess and asking advice on how to do various manoeuvres.' He replies tongue in cheek, and may one day add details about how to get the best from a Moggy. One lasting effect of his MM&TM days, apart from occasional live reunion concerts for Minor enthusiasts, was that he bought himself a Traveller.

The Minor's role in literature is still young and largely confined to technical books and histories such as this one. But there have been some interesting departures. One notable example is the story of JNX 13, an extremely sinister Morris Minor, which may alter future generations' perceptions of the 'dear little' car. It is the villain of *Beware the Morris Minor* by John Townsend, which appears in the spine-tingly section of Nelson Thornes' books for schools, along with a chiller about cannibal maggots and a spooky B&B called *The Sweet Dreams Guest House*. The series' declared aim is to alarm, thrill and encourage young secondary school students to pick up books again and again, and the synopsis of *Beware the Morris Minor* fits that bill:

> Our hero's life is about to end, yet he is only thirty years old. Following the death of his uncle, he inherits a car which has, he soon realises, disturbing powers. This clever and chilling story tells of the terrible havoc this ordinary Morris Minor can wreak. It is jinxed, and it has jinxed our hero . . .

Woooo! Maybe there was something occult at work when my bonnet flew off on Leeds ring road. Or maybe Townsend had chanced on the *Derby Trader* newspaper in March 1983 which reported that 19-year-old Diane Walmsley was giving away a Minor which her father had bought her as an incentive to pass her driving test. That worked, but not long afterwards, Diane heard spooky knuckles rapping at the side and rear windows. She bumped into things which hadn't seemed to be there – slowly, fortunately, and without getting hurt. Worst of all, she was spinning along Lime Grove in Chadderton when she felt a pair of hands grab her shoulders from the back seat, firmly but not forcibly – a description which sounds authentic. Thinking her little sister had stowed away secretly she called out: 'Rachel, don't be silly. Not when I'm driving.' But there was no reply, and when Diane braked, stopped and turned round, there was no one there . . . She went straight home and handed back the keys. Derbyshire police referred inquiries to the Driver Vehicle Licensing Centre in Swansea, who told the *Trader* the car's history 'would be looked at'. What they found about the past, I have not discovered, but the car's registration JRY 367E is still on record at the DVLA, albeit not renewed since 1987, so the car has been mothballed since then, unless it has gone into another dimension. It is also down officially as being painted a good colour for scary stories, bright red.

I am still hoping to find, and psychoanalyse, a teenager who has read not only *Beware the Morris Minor* but also, earlier in their school career, *Meet the Moggies*, a very different school book about a Minor, written by Rick Vanes with cheery pictures by David Birdsall. Aimed at primaries, it tells the story of Max, a four-door Minor 1000 which ends up in Mr Grubby's garage following an accident while pretending to be a racing car. No jinxes or evil eyes here. Max chums up with Marigold the kind old convertible, Mel the van and Mike the tow-truck, while also learning to face life's little challenges (so evident in any primary school playground) by dealing with Milo, a jealous old Morris Minor Traveller. This is much more in keeping with the cosy, upbeat tone of most written references to the car, which have a cosy, plucky feel, although often with elegiac intimations of the hard times so devastatingly portrayed by Martin Parr.

Pam Ayres is typical of this combination in her farewell poem to her own Minor, which faithfully carried her around for more than ninety thousand miles. She laments the way that faster, ruder modern traffic treats her car as an obstacle. If only she could repair it, or power it up a little, but even the simple mechanics of the Minor are beyond her. So is the likely bill if she took the car, her first and favourite, to one of the specialist renovation firms. And then there's the rust, and the dents, and the state of the seats . . . The strain runs through 'Goodbye, Worn-out Morris 1000' right from its title and opening line:

> Oh love, you've got no poke left.

to the last of ten increasingly doleful quatrains:

> But as I leave you in the scrapyard,
> Bangers piled up to the skies,
> Why do your rusty headlamps
> Look like sad, reproachful eyes?

Listen to Adrian May, on his CD 'Roadworks', singing 'Old Morris Minor', and you hear the same forlorn but fond effect as Pam's Oxfordshire lament. The recorded version starts with the 'trumpeting' of a Minor's exhaust, invokes William Blake's 'Jerusalem' by rhyming 'that wondrous motor of old' with the bow of burning gold, and ends with this ultimate wish:

If Christ revived, what would he drive, to make our
    road diviner?
I see him stuck in a queue on the M25
In his old Morris Minor.

Chorus: You loved your old Morris Minor
Trumpeting down memory lane . . .

In the world of art, the Morris Minor has a firm place in conventional car portraiture, a genre with many internet outlets for fond owners, as well as an honoured role in cartoons, especially of family outings and pastoral scenes. It has also played a part over the years in advertising for major organisations, especially comfortable state-run ones such as the old Gas and Milk Marketing Boards. More dynamically, the petrol company Shell used the car in a racing scene, scooting into the pits to have its windscreen wiped. National Westminster Bank then unfortunately undid the zippiness of that image in a TV commercial which showed a Minor falling slowly to pieces outside a branch.

This was in keeping, perhaps, with the Moggie's gentle

bit-part in the late twentieth century's salvation of historic architecture. Famously scruffy in his Minor convertible XPC 359G, the architectural critic of *The Sunday Times*, Ian Nairn, whom we have already met at Charlie Ware's workshop in Bath, tootled determinedly in the 1970s from building to threatened building. He was a sharp and witty journalist, referring to the elephant on the Albert Memorial as having 'a backside just like a businessman scrambling under a restaurant table for his cheque-book'. He was also hugely influential. For conservationists, Nairn's Morris Minor, usually parked outside the nearest pub, was the equivalent of the wagon train sighting the pennants of the US Cavalry.

At one stage, when he was recruited as co-author of the Surrey and Sussex volumes of the 47-volume *Survey of the Historic Buildings of England*, Nairn's little car formed a convoy with another carrying the august figure of Sir Nikolaus Pevsner, albeit only as a passenger. The great man's erudition and enthusiasm never extended to the internal combustion engine. His wife Lady Lola Pevsner, who now lies buried beside him in the village of Clyffe Pypard on the Wiltshire Ridgeway, drove him all over England after getting up early every day to make their packed lunches. In a Morris Minor? So legend has it, but this is another example of the wishful thinking shown in the TV portrait of the fellwalker Alfred Wainwright, which substituted a Minor for the Beetle he used in real life. Lady Pevsner preferred the Minor's relative, the Wolseley Hornet.

The Minor's own cosy 'heritage' nature might seem a

deterrent for contemporary artists, but one van bucked the trend in the hands of an artist from Jersey, Steph Newington. Painting the outside purple was perhaps a rather conventional statement, but the inside of her six-year project is something else. Now owned by Haynes Motor Museum in Somerset, but at the time of writing on show at the National Motor Museum in Beaulieu, Hampshire, the car provides an extraordinary canvas for Newington's skill. She bought it in 1994, when it was thirty-six years old, and stripped it down to individual components which were sandblasted, treated with anti-rust preservatives and then airbrushed – and we are talking about every single bolt and washer as well as the body panels. The *tour de force* is the underside, engine bay and several internal panels, which are painted to resemble wood, complete with knots and gargoyle-like faces. Padded button upholstery covers much of the rest of the interior, broken by elliptical paintings of underwater scenes, while the floor has a similarly elliptical panel, made of glass and hinged, which shows the wood effects and can be opened for a closer look. Parts of the chassis and suspension are marbled, and this technique has also been applied to voids of the alloy wheels and the repair jack. This is a car which might be envied even by Joanna Wood with her Hugh Mackay carpets and bespoke paintwork.

It was not, however, quite as cutting-edge as the Morris Minor performance art laid on by a group in London who were being monitored by potential funders and talent scouts in 1992. Lois Keidan's job, as Director of Live Arts at the

Institute of Contemporary Art in London at the time, was to keep an eye out for promising new work. Thus it was that she found herself watching eighteen elderly Morris Minors being lined up on Exchange Square in the City and linked to the office building Exchange House by streamers attached to their bumpers and wing mirrors. Some of the fluttering material soared up to the seventh storey and stretched for a hundred feet or more, until one of the six performance artists involved in the tableau started snipping at them with a large pair of scissors. This was the signal for five other members of the group to release the handbrakes of two of the lifeless cars and start pushing them in irregular loops round the next-door Broadgate shopping centre.

The old Andy Williams hit 'Almost There' crooned out loudly from amplifiers as these manoeuvres took place, and Keidan watched for half an hour. Then the two cars were allowed to collide gently, the brakes were put back on and the tableau was surrounded by the sort of hazard tape which traffic police use in road accidents. Up above, images of other Morris Minors were projected on to the office block's walls and windows. This was *Contra-Flow* by Housewatch, performance artists working with a £20,000 grant from the Arts Council, partly to pay for this and partly for another event. They could not have got by if Charlie Ware in Bath had not loaned them the eighteen cars for peanuts.

Was it art? Keidan told the *Independent* that she found the performance 'extraordinarily strong', although few ordinary members of the public lingered for the full half-hour. 'Morris Minors are so beautiful,' she said, and, if that was the work of Sir Alec Issigonis and his team, rather than Housewatch, the thought-provoking contrast of the old cars and their new setting was not.

> In this work you have to ask yourself what decrepit Morris Minors are doing in Broadgate, this pristine environment. It's the juxtaposition of battered cars against the bastion of capitalism and commerce. You do a double take. And it's the surprise, too, of seeing cars projected on to the seventh floor of Exchange House.

The strange tableau finally had a beauty in its ephemeral nature, she felt; in the fact that no one could buy it or hang it on their wall. A haunting impression of the Morris Minors may indeed have been left in the minds of some observers that would perhaps outlast metal and rubber and leather upholstery. But it was time for me to go in search of some more real cars.

Chapter 8
Beasts and Battlewagons

Magic of the mighty Minor – Car that drives Englishmen wild!

Headline, *The Sun*, 1983

 IT DOESN'T TAKE MUCH imagination to guess what people say to Mick Peeling when they see his monstrous red beast of a Morris Minor. 'Oh no! However could you do that to a Moggy?' he says, imitating hundreds of agonised cries at car shows or just on the road. 'They're always reading me the riot act – "What have you done?" . . . that sort of thing!' Peeling's warm West Country voice is full of glee as he recounts the reaction – usually adverse, occasionally hostile but always a reaction – which his customised creation inspires.

'That's the point, really,' says Mick, a former apprentice at Cowley who has run his own Morris Minor Clinic in Reading for forty-five years:

> It finally got to me ten years ago on the London-to-Brighton run, where I always take a few Morris Minors. My pride and joy was an immaculate white Traveller complete with light

wood, all original and absolutely spick and span inside. People would come up and have a polite look, nod their heads and go away satisfied that all was well. But where were the crowds? . . . They were gathered round these lads' customised Minors, sort-of half-finished things with huge engines. They were like wasps round jam.

Now it happened that Peeling's son and partner in the business, Jason, had just got married and gone on honeymoon at Daytona Beach in Florida.

He came back wide-eyed with tales of these Morris Minors – if you can call them that – stuffed with V8 engines and racing one another along the beach. 'Boy,' I said, 'You know what we've got to do?' The Big Red Beast was the result.

It started as a former police car, perfect underneath but with its bodywork ham-fistedly brush-painted over the usual sill and wheel-arch patches of rust. In went new mechanics (though all ex-BMC or British Leyland, nothing foreign or fancy), and on went the devilish red paint.

Then we were the bit of jam and we had the wasps. They was all around us, and a lot of them was slagging us off. But we had fifty or sixty phone calls at the garage the next week.

The car has operated since as a publicity generator, a regular at shows and a veteran of customised-versus-standard Morris Minor races. Tiff Nidell drove it for television's *Top Gear*, and Nigel Mansell had a tricky time keeping it under control on one of the circuits – it handles differently from a Formula One racing car. It has beef, though, according to Peeling. 'It did the fastest time round one track,' he says. His customers don't hold it against him, however disapproving they may be. 'They just say, "I hope you're not going to do that to my car", and I say, "Don't worry. The only thing I do for people like yourself is to make it safer."' If he installs a Marina 1300 engine, he adds disc brakes.

The beast also has a satellite navigation system inside, fancy seats and other gizmos which serve as a mobile advertisement for practical modernisations that can fit in an ordinary Minor. Mick learned his skills at Cowley, where his apprenticeship as a fitter and mechanic took him to the works – and the Morris Minor assembly line – one day a week. The idea was that he would gradually amass technical know-how to be put to use at the main dealers where he spent the other four days. Some of his friends went on to Cowley full time, others to Pressed Steel Fisher on the other side of the Oxford bypass, where they made the bodywork. Mick turned out to be 'the man who sorts the problems out'. His expertise was trouble-shooting in an era when car manufacture was nowhere near modern, computer-controlled standards.

The biggest problem was the 'Friday car'. One which didn't steer properly or had brakes which just weren't up to it.

They weren't mechanical faults, just the result of people rushing, because the 4 p.m. going-home time was getting near.

More regular faults tended to be in the gearbox, which was modified three times during the Minor's production life but still always had problems. It had no syncromesh on first gear, and so drivers had to stop to change or risk mechanical damage.

It's all very well putting that in the instruction book, but in reality . . . We had cars from schools of motoring whose gearboxes went down like wildfire. I remember one bringing us six busted ones in a week. Why Morris didn't put in synchro, I do not know.

It's a problem which persists. Mick was watching a Minor leave the yard just the week before we spoke when it made a noise like a shotgun going off.

He'd taken a whole tooth off first gear. I've another one in the yard now – chap was teaching his eighteen-year-old daughter, and she managed to break the whole mainshaft of the gearbox.

'Had she stopped?' I asked. 'Sort of . . . I think . . .' he said.

Peeling is sixty-eight and still going strong after starting with the main dealers when he left school at sixteen. 'The Minors won't let me retire,' he says. His latest modernisation is installing a Type Nine gearbox, as used in Ford Sierras.

> They're five-speed, and, to be honest, if you use them with the old engines the car tends to run out of puff. But put in a modern engine and brakes and you've got a very nice little modern car. She'll cruise comfortably on the motorway at 70 mph.

Comfortably but with the mild annoyance of causing more conventional motorists to feel they have to prove a point.

> We're just near the M4 here, and it's amazing how everyone races you on the motorway. The old 'Aaaah' factor disappears as drivers feel a surge: 'I'm not going to be overtaken by THAT.'

Souping up the engine of a Minor has a history going back almost to the car's first appearance, with early exponents including both Stirling and Pat Moss. The famous racing driver was not going to put up for long with a standard car and added a Derrington engine conversion to the one he briefly owned, a very early Series MM. It upped the car's power by 15 per cent, an increase outdone in his sister's convertible when Stirling's mechanic in 1954, Alf Francis, asked her if he could have a look at the workings of her first Minor, a side-valve convertible. When he returned it, the engine had a new aluminium head and a large SU carburettor and could manage a previously unimaginable

84 mph downhill and 72 on the flat. 'I started driving a bit quicker than I had been doing. I rather liked it,' says Pat in her autobiography *The Story So Far*. It struck her as a pity to have a car tuned by the country's best racing mechanic and not do anything about it, so that bit of customising is how the career of the world's best-known woman rally driver began.

She had a professional purpose, and so does Mick Peeling – for all its horrendous fuel consumption, his beast is a commercial product which gets his business known. Other customisers, the great majority, do it for the sheer exuberance. In the Minor they have a sturdy car to work on, and one with the sort of sweet and dainty reputation that brings a glint to the hot-rodder's evil eye. Hence the creation in New Zealand of the Bastardised Minor Club (adopting the old BMC initials deliberately to create a dark-side version of the – equally spoofy – Society for the Protection of Cruelty to Morris Minors, which Dave Plant launched in Cheshire in the 1980s). Its manifesto on the excellent Minor Mania website (www.minormania.com) states:

> The BMC was set up to protect the interests of NZ Minor Modifiers – the right to 'personalise' our Minors as we see fit and not to have to listen to the sermons of The Purists.

It arose in 1996 from a mixture of the usual debates between Fun Minor types and guardians of the Holy Minor at New Zealand's seventh National Morris Minor Convention, held at the mud-pool and geyser town of

Rotorua in the North Island's Bay of Plenty region. But it also included a robust anti-bureaucrat vein, an echo of Charles Ware's hopes for 'durable' Minors that could last for years. The manifesto continues:

> We, the Bastardisers, will ensure that the Minor continues on well into the next century. When the pathetic bunch of sops who call themselves politicians have finally legislated old cars off the road in this country, we, the Bastardisers, will have modified and improved our Minors so that they are eco-friendly and still more than a match for modern tin cans. The woofters in power will just have to put up with us.

So there! Members of the club, which has no golf-club rules or arduous qualifications – you just have to extreme-customise a Minor – can aim for a series of grades, of which the third and highest involves 'serious horsepower' and some sort of record of admiration from colleagues. Minor Mania suggests: 'Comments like "You are a real Bastardiser!" which let you know that you have reached the pinnacle of Minor Modification.' Who sits on this lofty spot? The highest scorers on 9.5 apiece are Paul Lopus of New York and Darryl Emmerson and Graham Powell in Britain, where the National Street Rod Association encouraged (and still encourages) such transformations as Bryan 'Golly' Godber's Havoc Morris Minor van, which at one stage went to an Arab sheikh who kept it lovingly in a garage in Mayfair, and 'Canned Heat', described by enthusiasts as 'a silver gasser with a blown Essex'. These competed gutsily with transformations of other marques, painted with shark's teeth and flames and carrying names such as 'Torque of the Devil' and 'Satan's Pawn'. Owners were often as wild as their cars, including The Who's explosives-obsessed drummer Keith Moon. In two cases, the competition between rival types of rodded car was complicated by forced marriages conducted with a welding torch. Half a Minor was fixed to half a VW Beetle in a mongrel called 'Push Me Pull You' and another was joined even more adventurously to half a Ford Capri. You may imagine Sir Alec Issigonis sending down curses from heaven, but . . . think again. He was the first person ever to cut a Minor in half, albeit lengthways. The rodders were front and back.

Sir Alec might also warm to a customised Minor called Noddy, which beneath its decorous red-and-yellow trim has a Mazda 3BT Rotary Turbo engine capable of reaching 110 mph in thirteen seconds. The car's livery is modelled on the classic Noddy car in which the boy with the bell-hat pootled about with Big Ears and Mr Plod, and which resembled a Morris Minor with its daffy smiling radiator and innocent eyes. A previously unrealised influence on Issigonis? Sadly no. The Minor appeared in 1948, and Noddy did not make his debut in print until the following year, with the book *Noddy and his Car* appearing only in 1951. But the two grew up together, along with my generation, and perhaps the similarity between the Minor and the Noddy car played a further part in the 'Love Bug' nature of the Minor which I discuss in Chapter One. After all, it was a standard joke among us kids that, from an early age, as young readers we had been encouraged to 'go to bed with Enid Blyton.'

The company of Bastardisers increases regularly on the Minor Mania website: the nearest thing they have to a clubhouse. Its virtual walls are lined with photos of their extraordinary transformations. Although it scores a relatively modest six points, I particularly like Richard and Joslyn Hobbs's purple 1960 four-door, which looks as though a basinful of cream has been tipped over it. Techies will love the way that the back doors have been welded shut, the roof sliced off and the sides lowered by three inches, but it is the pattern of cream paint dripping down the purple sides, bonnet and boot in big dollops which is really, prize-winningly original.

The Bastardiser judges clearly notch up most of their points in the hidden mechanics of these transformed cars. Hidden in most cases – top-scorer Paul Lopus actually has his gleaming Chevy 350cid engine with its Weiand blower towering out of its bonnet-less compartment, mounted on a platform like silverware on a golfer's mantelpiece and contrasting brilliantly with the Minor's scarlet body paint. That gets the 9.5 rating – and good luck to Lopus, who spent four years building the thing. But spare a thought for poor Dave Marshall, whose 'Bloody Grinner' customised Minor wins only four points: its fine combination of flames streaming back along the bonnet and wings from a radiator with shark's teeth painted (and cut) in a crooked grin cannot compensate for standard mechanics inside.

The engineering inventiveness of Bastardisers is endless. A Traveller body is mounted on a shortened Mazda pick-up truck's frame plus part of an old Ford. Or an elderly 1954 two-door sits on a Suzuki Samurai 4×4 frame, with power provided by a computer-controlled Chevy V6 with overdrive. This blew the four-wheel-drive facility originally inherited with the 4×4 frame by Nick Harvey, the American enthusiast who built this car. But he plans to get it going again. The joy of hobby engineering shines through entry after entry: just how much more can we get mongrel, tortured and twisted moving components to do?

There's also another dynamic at work: a cheeky pleasure in knowing that the much larger corps of fellow enthusiasts for Minors, the ones who like their cars perfect and exactly restored, will mostly be aghast at bastardisations. Irene Heath from Worcestershire may sound like the classic Minor owner, with her standard 1965 C-reg called Felicity, which she retired from her motorway commute into Birmingham because the old girl was no longer up to it. But Felicity is booked to get teeth as crooked and grinning as Dave Marshall's flames-and-sharks car. Heath tells other Bastardisers: 'By the time she's done, purists will take one look and have heart failure (I hope).' New engine, gearbox and above all a dark blue livery painted with silver dragons should do the trick. Another applicant for club membership, whose Minor is a modest-looking affair but full of non-original parts which offend absolutist restorers, pleads: 'The classic car buffs dismiss me, and I was hoping for some recognition among yourselves as a Minor bastard. For this I would be more than happy to purchase a T-shirt and wear it proudly to every Morris gathering in South East England.'

It would be hard to be curmudgeonly about some of the truly exceptional flights of fancy in the customised Minor world. The creations of the Beardmore brothers, John and Robin, are breathtaking feats of car engineering, not surprising from a workshop that produced a V8-powered Reliant Kitten. If you want a spotless restoration of a rare, rubber-winged Minor Post Office van, or a Mazda MX5 transformed into a Moggy, they are the people for you. Myself, I specially like their half-size, precisely-scaled version of Robin's Minor pick-up, painted pink, and also the radio-controlled model Minor which they made from a fibreglass mould of a pottery ornament of the car. But what can match the lobster-shaped Morris Minor which brought its co-creator Phil Vincent into conflict with the Chief Constable of Nottinghamshire twenty years ago? Bright red and with a five-foot tail and working claws, this is the weirdest of the many strange customised Moggies that have gone beyond their creators' imaginations and actually taken to the roads. It was created for a very strange children's TV programme but its later career was equally odd.

Shoving away two obstreperous dogs at his Morris Minor specialist garage in Sibthorpe, near Newark, Phil Vincent explains how a friend was contacted in 1987 by a TV company who needed a VW Beetle turned into a mechanical lobster, fast.

He asked them why, and they said it was a series all about some architecture bloke called Professor Lobster visiting interesting buildings like the Albert Hall and the Clifton suspension bridge. My mate, bless him, said: 'You don't want a Beetle for that, you need a Morris Minor.' The bloke got on to me, and I knew a woman who couldn't drive but had ended up for some reason with a 1966 Minor and wanted it off her hands, so we could start work straight away.

And that was how Phil and his dad Eric and uncle Henry, who together ran Henric Minor Specialists, famed at the time for gold-standard new body panels, got to build the lobster Morris. Its doors were valanced at the base – the old rust trap – like the edge of a lobster's shell, the segmented tail curled up from the boot and the claws were operated by a small electric motor concealed below an old motorbike helmet which made the creature's head.

The TV company was delighted, and *Professor Lobster* duly ran for six episodes in 1987–8, with the eminent Professor Ken Martin from the Royal Institute of British Architects driving it cheerfully into a studio packed with children before discoursing on the building trade. His appearance, not only in the wacky car but wearing vivid dungarees was greeted by the programme's theme song:

> There's a wise old man at the bottom of the sea
> He's come to help both you and me

with its rousing chorus of 'Professor Lobster!'

The idea was to draw children in to the possibly boring-sounding subject of architecture, and it seems to have worked, although not enough to convince the broadcasters to show a second series. Ken Martin, a distinctive figure with wild hair and a Lancashire accent, recalls that the lobster gave a smooth and easy ride, with ample visibility between the claws. 'I pressed a little button to open and shut them,' he said, a feat he performed while driving across the dizzy span of the Clifton suspension bridge in Bristol.

> The children seemed to enjoy it, and it served to link the programme's different subjects together. I still get people coming up to me now and then and saying, 'Are you Professor Lobster?'

Most architects have interesting views on design, and Martin, who headed the Liverpool Polytechnic school of architecture for sixteen years, greatly approves of the lobster car's 'good balance and great sense of colour'. As for the Minor more generally, he echoes many other expert comments by calling it 'classic, modest and practical – like a good vernacular English village building'.

When the programmes were over, Phil Vincent made an offer of £1,000 to buy back the car, and it was put to work as a mobile advertisement for Henric, just as the Beast has publicised Mick Peeling's Morris Minor centre in Reading. 'I used it to go shopping as well, which was funny,' says Phil, 'and I taxed it as a straightforward Morris, not a lobster.' But then pride intervened, with its notorious consequences. Phil and the lobster were asked to take part in the Lord Mayor of London's show, and while parading through the capital's streets they were spotted by an excessively conscientious road safety officer. Unaware of this, the lobster cruised back up the A1 as uneventfully as it had travelled down, with the engine's governor keeping its speed to a maximum of 50 mph, preventing any naughty thoughts of astonishing a Porsche or Mercedes Benz with the sight of a big red crustacean zooming past.

> But back home at Sibthorpe the village bobby comes up and says, 'I'm sorry Mr Vincent but we've got to impound your lobster. They don't think it's safe.'

It turned out that the safety officer had been involved in a case where stanchions holding an emblem on a Jaguar had failed, and the lobster's claws were just too much for him.

Vincent rang the Chief Constable of Nottinghamshire:

'But look, I'm using this to raise money for Children in Need.'

'Mr Vincent, it could well be children who don't see your lobster's claws.'

'What, not see my bright red lobster car?' asked Phil, incredulously.

'Mr Vincent,' came the reply, 'there are 250 buses in Nottingham and they are a lot bigger and more obvious than your lobster. But five people get knocked down by them every month.' (Or words to that effect.)

The lobster was grounded, and in due course Phil sold it to a buyer in the North, where it has since disappeared from Morris Minor enthusiasts' radar. But not before it had had one last fling. The lobster entered the annual Wacky Races meet at the Unbarring in Germany. 'It was the trip from Hell,' says Phil, who, by towing the lobster behind his 1969 Morris Minor van, piloted a sort of Morris Minor version of a bendy bus across Europe to the famous track between Cologne and Mainz. 'We hit a juggernaut, got lost in Brussels and ran out of money.' But the lobster made it, raced and got safely home before going . . . well, to pot.

Phil's strange car and its motorised nippers never saw serious action, but large numbers of other Morris Minors were designed to do so. The Government was a regular customer at Cowley, especially for Travellers, which were ordered by the Ministries of Agriculture, Employment and Health, the Home Office, Customs and Excise and especially the Ministry of Defence. Thus began another unlikely chapter in the history of the cosy and peaceful vicar's runabout, although it retained an appropriately English tone. The commonest image of a Tilly, as military Minors were known (a short form of their official name: Car Utility 4×2 Morris 1000), is of a crisply-uniformed woman driver saluting her officer passenger. In a film she would be played by Jenny Agutter or Honeysuckle Weeks.

Some 2,000 Minors were deployed by the three armed services between 1966 and 1980, when the last was replaced by one of the new fleet of Ford Escorts and Vauxhall Chevettes which took on the Tilly jobs. The Army cars were olive green, often with matching interior trims in the pleasantly-named, traditional Minor colours of Autumn

Leaf or Porcelain Green. Royal Air Force cars were blue-grey, and Naval Travellers, naturally, were Navy Blue. The Naval ones were the most-travelled, in accordance with the old recruiting slogan 'Join the Navy and see the world.' Every aircraft carrier had a Traveller or two on board for use as a runabout in foreign ports and a modified tropical version of the car, done in-house by the services, had slightly improved ventilation and sometimes included extra opening windows. These Minors were often redecorated in white, like their users who swapped khaki for tropical-issue shorts or ducks.

There were no great heroics, but Minors served in several potential tight spots, including Aden and Northern Ireland, where specially-shaped wire mesh panels were available to fit to Traveller windows and front and rear lights. The RAF had one in the Maldives, and there were small fleets at British bases in Cyprus and Germany, where Tilly jobs punctuated the boredom of the long-term alert against a Cold War threat that, in the event, never materialised. The Jennies and Honeysuckles drove officers and chaplains around, the military police equipped their Travellers with bubbletops and flashing blue lights, vehicles stationed on airfields had bright yellow roofs to help visibility if they ventured on to runways. The official purpose of the Tillies was described by the Ministry of Defence as 'carrying two persons or four persons and a full load of stores' and that was the backbone of their job. Donkey Work. A jeep without the 4×4 ability to go offroad.

The most interesting Traveller encounter with the

military that I know of, however, happened to a civilian car: the 1963 Rose Taupe Traveller that Roger Wolstenholme from Halifax used when installing milking parlours in state farms behind the Iron Curtain. In 1968 he was travelling between sites in the Tatra mountains in southern Poland and was surprised at the enormous number of tanks and other military vehicles, plus columns of soldiers, all sheltered in woods or under camouflage netting close to the Czech border. Events involving the independently minded Dubcek government in Prague were moving towards a crisis, and when Wolstenholme crossed back into West Germany at Helmstedt, he was taken aside by an intelligence officer from the British Army. 'Noticed anything unusual, old boy?' His revelation of the colourful details of the build-up in the Tatras were greeted with incredulity: 'The "intelligence" officer told me I needed to get help for what he called my hysterical imagination.'

There are plenty of service Travellers still around and in good condition, as particular favourites with Minor restorers, who have endless little details to forage for in an ex-military vehicle. You can scrub up the point on the bumper valance where the regimental crest was fixed or rub your finger in the rivet holes under the bonnet on the right hand side where the Ministry of Defence put its special identity plate. There could be a fire extinguisher bracket in the front footwell, and cars with engines reconditioned while in military service may have traces of duck-egg blue on the engine mounting, which showed that the work had been carried out. Most treasured, perhaps, are olive green

Army Travellers with red-painted wings, which came the closest to danger of all the fleet. They were used by Bomb Disposal teams.

The collectible status of these cars is not shared by a Morris Minor whose name became tragically associated with cruelty, violence and injustice, the very opposites of the cuddly and lovable image which enfolds the car. This was a 1956 saloon painted grey, registration number 847 BHN, and it appeared all over the newspapers in August 1961, five years after leaving Cowley. The car belonged to a scientist at the Government's Road Research Laboratory, Michael Gregsten, thirty-six, a married father of two who was unhappy with life at home. He was having an affair with a young colleague at the lab, Valerie Storie, twenty-two. Her name will instantly link the car for many to the A6 Murder trial, the subsequent execution of James Hanratty, and one of the most celebrated campaigns against a supposed mis-carriage of justice of recent times.

The couple were making love in the Minor in a field near Dorney on the Thames west of London, a beautiful oasis of countryside, steeped in history: Dorney Court, where the first pineapple in Britain was grown, is just down the road, and Dorneywood, the official residence of Home Secretaries, is not far away. It was only 9.30 in the evening when a man tapped on the car window and then, when Gregsten opened the door, confronted the couple with a handgun. For the next four hours, Gregsten and Storie endured a nightmare of inexplicable behaviour, first lectured by the man in his sharp Cockney accent, or enduring his silence as the three of them sat in the car in the field for almost two hours. Then Gregsten was made to drive round North London, stopping at one point to pick up a pint of milk from a vending machine. Finally, the gunman ordered a change of direction. The car headed north, up the A6 into Bedfordshire, before doing a U-turn and parking in a lay-by known by grim coincidence as Deadman's Hill. Here Gregsten was shot dead in front of Storie, who was then raped on the back seat before bizarrely being asked by the killer to give him a basic lesson in driving the car. Once satisfied, he ordered her out and shot her five times as she pleaded pitifully for life and offered him a £1 note – all the money she had. The car screeched off and lurched away towards London.

Astonishingly, Storie was not dead. She could scarcely move, but she survived her wounds for three hours until a farm worker found her, and the dreadful story became national news. Hanratty, a twenty-five-year-old petty criminal from London who had spent most of the previous seven years in jail, was quickly on detectives' wanted list because of an Identikit image and voice description drawn from Storie's evidence, and also because he had disappeared. He was arrested in October 1961 in Blackpool and convicted of murder at Bedford Assizes the following February. The appeal was dismissed in March, and he was hanged on 4 April 1962 at Bedford jail.

Capital punishment was not abolished in Britain for another four years, but by 1961 there were routine, large-scale protests against executions, and only six more people were subsequently hanged. More than 28,000 people signed a petition asking for Hanratty's sentence to be commuted to life imprisonment, in spite of the chilling nature of the crime and the pitiful sight of Storie paralysed for life from the waist down. She was taken into court on a stretcher to give the damning evidence, drawn from her five-and-a-half hours of terror with the killer in the little car. After the hanging, these protests developed into something more significant. In the skilful hands of investigative journalists, including Paul Foot and Bob Woffinden, the case became the best-known example in the country of alleged injustice, sloppy police work and hurried legal processes. Alibi witnesses were produced to say that Hanratty had spent the murder evening and night at a guesthouse in Rhyl, north Wales, and an alternative possible killer, Peter Alphon, was put in the frame. He was another petty criminal from London who had been the police's first suspect. The campaign was not only persuasive but an early example of celebrity PR. John Lennon lent his Rolls Royce for the Hanratty family to visit the lay-by at Deadman's Hill, and famous modern legal reputations enhanced by involvement included those of Lord Chief Justice Lane, Geoffrey Bindman and Michael Mansfield. None of a string of appeals and inquiries has overturned the verdict, and in 2002 the revolutionary skills of DNA tracing appeared to establish Hanratty's guilt conclusively. Semen from the rape and a handkerchief wrapped round the murder revolver was linked to DNA extracted from his exhumed corpse. The chances of a misidentification were said by experts to be a billion to one against, and that was the view of the Appeal Court. Paul Foot remained unconvinced, because of the fourteen witnesses who had told him with varying degrees of detail that Hanratty had been in Rhyl, and because of the chance that DNA evidence had been contaminated. But the combined and considerable intellects of Lord Chief Justice Woolf, Lord Justice Mantell and Mr Justice Leveson ruled otherwise, and there the matter lies.

But what of the role of 847 BHN in this dreadful story? Both the trial and the justice campaign were naturally focused on the evidence of Valerie Storie and the Rhyl alibi, but the Morris Minor was important too. The prosecution produced a witness, John Silkett, who identified Hanratty as the driver of a grey Morris Minor 'speeding' along Eastern Avenue in east London in the early morning, hours after the murder. A second witness, James Trower, also swore that Hanratty was the man at the wheel of a grey Minor as it turned into Redbridge Lane, close to Avondale Crescent, the side street behind Redbridge police station where it was found abandoned. As it happened, both men were with companions who disagreed with them, and the second sighting was complicated by the fact that a woman who lived in Avondale Crescent also owned a grey Morris Minor.

Once the miscarriage of justice campaign got into its stride, it further emerged that sightings of the car on the morning after the murder had come from as far away as Matlock in Derbyshire. These might have been mistaken, just as Silkett and Trower may have been, but the fact that they were not disclosed to the defence by the prosecution at the trial naturally created suspicion. Calculations were made involving the mileage on the Minor's instruments and the distance it might have travelled after the murder. The more extreme sceptics suggested that it took so long to reach Redbridge that it must have been driven all the way in reverse gear.

In a wider sense, the role of the Minor is potentially interesting too. One of the features of the A6 Murder was the level of public outrage at the time, which later played a part in the arguments put forward by those convinced that Hanratty was innocent. Murder in Britain is seldom random, and even more rarely is it so sadistically cruel. It was extremely important for the police to catch the killer, and there was intense pressure on them to do so. Did that lead to the cutting of corners, such as the failure to disclose the other, alleged Morris Minor sightings? Paul Foot and Bob Woffinden suspected that it might have done.

Part of this public reaction involved the car. Not only had every standard of decency been violated but the rape and murder had taken place in the cosy runabout with which everyone was so familiar and so at ease. Gregsten's modest choice of a Minor was typical of so many unpretentious 'ordinary' people at the time: an extension of Everyman and Everywoman's domestic ideal of a small house with a manageable garden and two children. If he had been going behind his family's back with his mistress in a Bentley, the public would still have been revolted by the murder and rape, but not to quite the same extent, delicate as the nuance might have been. In those different days, knowledge of the two victims' affair would have affected the views of most people in the same, subtle way. But this information was not disclosed until some years later; at the time, the victims were simply two hard-working ordinary colleagues attacked by Evil in the nation's favourite car.

None of this is to moderate the horror of what happened, or to try to build a fanciful theory on something too dreadful to carry such a lightweight structure. You need only to look at the court photographs of detectives examining the abandoned car to see what I mean. In the dusk, illuminated by floodlights, the Morris tilts at an angle on the pavement with its offside wheels in the gutter and its rear wing perilously close to a garden wall and a cherry tree. No 1960s Morris Minor owner would normally leave a car like that. It has its fixed 'smiling face' of radiator grille, headlamps and bonnet, and behind it there is an even more innocuous looking Austin A35. But everywhere police stand in knots.

There are strange sides, customised sides and military sides to the Morris Minor's long history. This is the dark side, and you cannot fail to be appalled.

Chapter 9
To Boldly Go

All along your sides and middle
You are turning rusty brown,
Though you took me ninety thousand miles
And never let me down.

Pam Ayres, 'Goodbye, Worn-out Morris 1000'

 THERE ARE PLENTY OF places more exciting than Haslemere, but on the forecourt of a pleasant family house in the Surrey town stands one of the most adventurous Morris Minors in the world. A demure 1951 saloon with a pattern of daisy transfers on its doors and wings, the little car looks like a student runabout. But if MYD 633, formerly known as Matilda, could speak, she would tell you tales of the blue men of the Atlas mountains, Atlantic rollers crashing on to the yellow beaches of Dakar, and an evening of beer and Trivial Pursuits at the English Pub in Ulan Bator's main square.

'Never!' says Alison Morrell, who was baking a cake when I rang in May 2008 to tell her what had happened to the old banger she had last seen in the summer of 2004. Matilda was a non-runner by then, after the standard Morris

Minor life of tootling Alison from her home in Alconbury to work as a PA in Huntingdon, and in between times teaching the family's children to drive. The Morrells finally decided to put her on eBay, and she went for £410 – rather less in real terms than Alison paid when she bought her from Mr Mark Dexter of Peterborough in 1978 (£357, equivalent to £1,415 in 2004).

Matilda had exercised the usual Morris Minor hold on the Morrells, sentiment triumphing for two decades over practicality and cost. Alison's husband served in the RAF, and for many years after she broke down in the mid-1980s and was mothballed, Matilda was discreetly stored in a series of hangars alongside the country's latest warplanes. 'She was a marvellous old car,' Alison reminisced before getting back to her butter and flour. 'But she sometimes used to fill up with black smoke, and then she stopped altogether. Eventually I thought: I could have a car that actually works, instead of this thing.'

Little did she know that Matilda was about to get a tiger beneath her bonnet. The successful eBay bid came from an enterprising businessman, Tony Manos, a former technical journalist who still has a yen for the buccaneering side of his old trade. He was looking for a challenge, something different from his conventional travels between Haslemere and London, when he saw an advertisement for an amateurs' rally from the old Brooklands racing circuit to Dakar in Senegal; any car could enter. What sort, wondered Tony, would be really cool? He promptly went on eBay, and within a month his brother-in-law collected Matilda from Huntingdon, did a bit of a clean-up and fitted a new battery at his home near Wisbech. Then he turned the key and the engine started first time.

So began Matilda's new life, following a tradition already well established by the time her first owner, Robert Braybrooke of Minehead, took her on the road after paying his licence fee of £17 7s 6d (£375 today). The 'rally boys' had long been racing cars for manufacturers, both to test out their limits and to give more mundane drivers a sense that their everyday runabout had a tiger beneath the bonnet. (My *Guardian* colleague Enid Wilson, the Lake District country diarist, was taken as ballast as a schoolgirl when her father test-drove Austins and Morrises up the Hard Knott and Wrynose passes in the 1920s to supplement his income as a photographer.) The Minor's sturdiness made it a natural target for these sporting drivers, and such activities became big business after Austin and Morris merged into the British Motor Corporation, and the Competition Shop was set up at Abingdon to fine-tune cars for high-profile races and rallies. These got all the publicity associated with motor sport as well showing how well and – particularly in the Minor's case – how reliably the cars could perform. After a terrible season at Le Mans in 1955, when the world's worst motor-racing accident saw 80 spectators killed after a Mercedes crashed into a grandstand, BMC decided to concentrate only on rallies.

In keeping with the Minor's image, the first and most successful rally car was called Granny: a souped-up light green two-door driven by Pat Moss, the show jumper and sister of Sir Stirling Moss (who shared her love of speed and had a very early Series MM Minor of his own). For three years between 1957 and 1960, she hurled NMO 933 round the worst challenges that the rally circuit could offer, failing to finish only once, when the car slithered off a snowy road en route to Monte Carlo and whacked into a concrete post. In her book *The Story So Far*, Pat Moss describes Granny as 'the most fantastic, incredible car I have ever driven'. She rallied it for an unprecedented four seasons, at a time when it was almost unheard-of for a car to last a year on the taxing routes, and it motored on long after other cars of its age had fallen apart. 'It seemed to be unbreakable. I always asked for the same one again because it was so good and so reliable.'

Her adventures in a Minor began in 1954 with a 'scavenger hunt' organised by Harrow Car Club, in which drivers whizzed around country lanes trying to find a list of trophies, including a feather, an old newspaper and a worm. Pat teamed up with a horse-riding friend Ann Wisdom, appropriately known as Wiz, and was soon tackling more complicated challenges. On the celebrated Hants and Berks Experts Night Rally, one of those English oddities for enthusiasts that take place when the rest of us are asleep, she and Wiz had to track down marshals who were hidden in woods, an underground stream (which drivers had to access in a coracle) and disguised as one half of a couple in a lovers' lane, parked beside decoy couples and also genuine ones, although most of the latter naturally melted away as more and more rally drivers banged on their windows to ask if one of them was the race marshal.

Pat and Stirling's parents were both amateur rally drivers and car enthusiasts, and they planned to give their daughter a Morris Minor as soon as she turned seventeen in 1952. Stirling had by then been the proud owner of a unique stripped-down Austin Seven since the age of nine. Known as 'the Jeep', because it had no bodywork and just two seats perched at the front, it taught him the basic skills which he later put to such famous use, as he careered around the family's ten-acre garden at Bray, near Maidenhead, where they lived in a house built on stilts because of flooding.

The Minor was less easy to come by than an ancient Austin. There was such a long waiting list that the Mosses settled for a 1936 Morris Ten, and it was not until the end of the year that a smart grey Minor convertible, one of the early models with a side-valve engine, was delivered. Pat was still primarily interested in her show jumping, riding with the British national team and winning cupboardfuls of trophies at local shows – forty prizes from twenty-seven events in 1953. But the much greater power and sophistication of the Minor started something. After all, she was Stirling Moss's sister. And her father, who had finished thirteenth in the 1924 Indianapolis during time off from running his chain of London dental surgeries, sensed her natural ability in advanced driving lessons which they did together. He taught her to heel-and-toe, a racing driver's trick of using one foot simultaneously to brake and double-declutch down the gears, using the ball of the foot on the brake and a flick of the heel on the accelerator.

Pat's show-jumping career continued to flourish, but it was a seasonal sport, ending in October, and she realised that rallying cars could be an excellent way to spend her spare time. She had a car; she had traded-in her Minor for £450 (£8,700 today) and bought an £800 Triumph TR Sports, selling her father a half-share in her latest mount, Ricochet, to cover the balance. But she needed expenses to tackle the big European rallies, so she approached Triumph and asked if she could drive for them on this basis. They didn't bite, and that (as the then head of BMC's Competition Shop, Marcus Chambers, chortled for many years afterwards) was how Stirling Moss's sister slipped through his great rival's fingers and into his. Pat's father had a friend at BMC who immediately realised the PR potential of a Moss in their rallying team: publicity for their cars was the whole point of taking part in rallies for motor manufacturers. With Pat secured, BMC even based their new team badge, and ultimately the company logo, on her show jumping prize rosettes and adopted the Continental usage 'écurie' (French for 'stable') to described the 1955 team.

Moss was allocated NMO 933, which had been used in just one rally by the future chief constable of Northamptonshire, John Gott, who led the BMC rally team when not on duty as a police officer. Chambers and his colleagues were prepared for Pat to be a bit of a token, plucky but inexperienced, but she removed any doubts about her driving straight away. After what she modestly called 'a nasty moment' overtaking a Mercedes on her first outing, her car was nicknamed the 'Mercedes Minor.' A second nasty moment soon afterwards, involving a minibus, extended the name to the 'Mercedes Minor Minibus'. This was far too cumbersome and was soon shortened to 'Mini' (which may have been one influence in the naming of Issigonis's second great creation, the Mini Minor).

Pat and Mini – whose name was changed to Granny in her second year of rallying, out of respect for her age – really established the Minor's reputation as a car that would take almost any amount of knocks. In a more modest way a four-door grey Minor, NJB 277, also played a part. Because Mini/Granny was being used by Gott again in the freezing, snowbound Tulip rally in the Low Countries in 1955, Pat and Wiz entered in the four-door and never forgot the experience. The extra doors added weight, which BMC compensated for by taking out the heater, so the young women's breath froze on the inside of the windows, and the clatter of the engine on rough stretches was echoed by their chattering teeth. But they finished, and their Minor needed minimal maintenance. The rallying world was taking an interest.

The big test came with an unusual event called the Liège-Rome-Liège rally (which neither started in Liège nor visited Rome). Abandoned long ago because of modern safety standards, it took cars along hideous roads between Belgium and what was then Yugoslavia on a timetable which made nonsense of several countries' speed laws. Minimal checks were made on the cars' equipment and safety, and each team of two had to keep on the go for ninety-six hours with just a handful of one-hour breaks. It was the daddy of all rallies, says Pat, a flat-out belt across Europe with 'no silly regulations'. She was so tired by Yugoslavia that she kept seeing black cats crossing the road ahead, while Wiz had visions of burning cars in the Minor's path and tried to stop Pat hitting them until both realised that, dopy with fatigue, they were seeing things.

No car as small as a Minor had ever finished the Liège, but Granny roared in twenty-third in the overall field and, in the Ladies' section, second only to an MGA sports car. She survived the treacherous gravel of the 8,000-ft Gavia pass in the Alps – a military road where the sight of the rally so absorbed an Italian general watching troop manoeuvres from a helicopter that he fell out (luckily landing in thick bushes) – escaping damage from a leap so high above a dirt road gully that the car behind saw the one ahead clear beneath Pat and Wiz's wheels. Two nuts held a rear wheel on during a ten-minute nightmare on an Italian autostrada, where successive bangs, as metal sheared, reminded the pair of the Blitz. According to Mark Chambers, Pat's mother kept ringing up BMC to demand: 'Stop the girls. It's too dangerous. Make them stop.'

None of this dented Pat's élan, any more than immersion in a sort of fruit cocktail when the Minor landed heavily after a bump saw the entire car leave the ground before crashing back. Dozens of oranges and apples from the drivers' food box smashed into the roof and were turned into pulp. The next year, Granny was entered for the most coveted rally of all, the Monte Carlo, but this time she met an obstacle which even a Morris Minor could not overcome. Pat and Wiz had been leap-frogging with a rival car for miles when they lost control in thick snow on a right-hand bend. The car ploughed straight on into a snowdrift which would have been fine, had not the village's only concrete bollard been concealed inside it. Granny smacked straight into it, and both women cracked their heads on the sun visor, Pat staggering out with blood streaming down her face, while Wiz was semi-conscious. Luckily Pat's cut proved to be superficial, and Wiz came round to find a cross-eyed monk from a nearby abbey bending over her to help. Briefly thinking she was dead, she remembers being surprised that even in Heaven, people could have cross-eyes.

Granny's fan had been knocked into the radiator, but the car was patched up next morning by the BMC back-up team, and she made it to Monte Carlo, where only one of the starters from Paris had managed to finish inside the official time. Far from denting the Minor's reputation, the near-disaster only added more lustre. 'They go on and on,' said Pat. 'They take the most amazing punishment. And they are so simple for the mechanics to mend afterwards.'

Bigger, faster and more sporty cars were to figure in her later rallying career, but Pat had one more adventure in Granny and one which struck a chord with me. As a young reporter, I was rash enough on holiday in the Lake District to tackle the Hard Knott pass in PMV 143 with five friends. As we ground up the evilly-steep zigzags from Eskdale, the air inside the car filled with the sweet but sinister smell of clutch fluid, soured by metal over-heating and with a descant of shrill advice from the back. On the very last slope we seemed to have had it, with a dreadful bit of reversing the only way back. But I had been to a rowing school and remembered the coach's shouts of 'Swing together' from the towpath and the effect on the momentum of a racing eight. 'Swing together!' I shouted, and everyone did. It may only have been psychological, but the rhythm seemed to heave the Minor over the final hundred yards to a gasping halt at the summit.

Pat's memory was of going down the pass – watching from Granny as a novice rally driver in a Morris Traveller kept braking at the wrong moment until the car went into a spin. Clinging to the mountain in a series of narrow shelves, the Hard Knott is absolutely no place for that sort of thing, especially when the Traveller ended up facing the wrong way and began to slide down towards Little Langdale backwards. Pat saw the passenger door open, and the navigator jumped out, but the young driver bravely stayed on his equivalent of the burning deck and somehow steered backwards to the bottom and into a snowdrift. He got the car out and facing the right way again, but the whey-faced navigator refused to get back in. After all, the equally dreadful Wrynose Pass lay just ahead.

Granny worked between rallies as a runabout for mechanics and kept going as a BMC racer until 1960, when she was finally sold. Some five years later Pat saw her again at White City in London, where she was show-jumping, and offered to buy her. The owner, who used the car daily for his ordinary travelling, wanted more than she was prepared to pay, so instead she invested in a painting of the battling old Minor being driven by her husband, rally driver Erik Carlsson, flying round a corner with all four wheels off the ground. She hung this on their dining room wall and, after her retirement from rallying, contented herself with a 1966 convertible in dark green which she drove more sedately at home.

Just a year later, a black saloon with an exotic future came off the Morris Minor assembly line and went to another distinguished home. For thirteen years UYU 741F served as the chauffeur-driven London runabout of the Archbishop of Canterbury, clocking up only 18,000 miles. It had four owners, all archbishops and all claiming to have stuck to a rule that the little car was not to be used in the rain. So when it came up for sale in early 1980, after the Rt Rev. Dr Robert Runcie opted for something bigger and ordered an Austin Maxi, it was understandably billed in Nigel Dempster's *Daily Mail* gossip column as the best Morris Minor in the country.

That day the editor of *Sporting Cars*, Philip Young, was on a train from Malvern to London and chanced to swap his *Mail* for a copy of *The Times* which a clergyman sitting opposite him had been reading. As the train made its way through the Cotswolds, they got chatting, and the clergyman, who introduced himself as the Archdeacon of Daventry, pointed out the paragraph about the car. Wouldn't it be good, he mused, if the sale could be used to further publicise the church's work and raise money for good causes? Young for his part had just been reading an article in *Motoring News* about plans to hold India's first car rally through a mixture of jungle, desert and the Himalayas. An idea formed. A few days later, he went to see the writer and journalist Gerry Phillips, who was in charge of drawing up the Indian rally route, and asked him what sort of car would be best suited to its challenges. Young remembered the answer well enough to put it down verbatim in his book *The Himalayan Minor*: 'Something not too big, sort of Escort size, but as strong as a tank and as reliable as a Morris Minor.'

Some months and many meetings with the Church Commissioners later, Young found himself at Lambeth looking over the spotless, Trafalgar Blue UYU 741F, with its handy four doors, original pale blue upholstery and a tool box which had never been used. The battery was flat, as any owner of a Minor left unused for a few weeks would expect, but remarkably – and apparently proof of the rain driving ban – there was no rust on the bodywork. A deal to buy it for £2,000 (£6,000 today and pretty much top whack at the time) was concluded, with Lord Montagu of Beaulieu putting up the money and offering a place for the car in his National Motor Museum if and when it returned. It would not be so pristine after thousands of miles on Indian tracks, but the curiosity value of a strange and historic achievement was thought to make up for that.

There were some interesting problems as the car was prepared for its new life at the special tuning workshops of British Leyland's Competitions Department in Abingdon. The appealing curves of the Minor affected almost every surface and caused problems for Unipart's sponsorship transfers. Beneath the bonnet and under the chassis all manner of strengthenings took place; an Austin Healey Sprite engine was fitted, raising the capacity from a standard 1098cc to 1275cc, the back seat was taken out and, most significantly for any Minor owner, the growly phut-phut of the exhaust was quietened, because noise adds to rally drivers' fatigue. One last but vital addition remained: a co-driver. The Rev. Rupert Jones, vicar of All Saints in Rochdale, was taken on board, for practical as well as spiritual reasons. A rally veteran who had set speed records for the Austin A35 and done the Monte Carlo in a Mini, he was nicknamed 'Jehu' by motoring journalist Philip Llewellin, after the Old Testament king of Israel whose furious chariot-driving is described in 2 Kings 9: 20. Thinking of India, Young also knew that Jones had survived the boiling heat of Liège in temperatures that had sent his co-driver, John Gott, nearly delirious from sunstroke.

The Himalayan rally was seen off from Bombay in the summer heat by a crowd of more than a million sightseers, with the Minor at the end of a line of sixty-seven entrants which took over an hour to get away. There had been last preliminaries in Britain, including a blessing from Dr Runcie, who gamely took his extraordinarily adapted runabout for a sedate circle round the Lambeth Palace fountain. The polite jokes about the radiator containing holy water began to seem apt when the very first day of the rally saw a clutch of cars, including an Alfa which had been favourite in the Minor's small-car class, crash out in a series of mechanical breakdowns and pile-ups. Young and Jones did excellently on the twisty, narrow roads to Poona, out-running bigger rivals, including a Mercedes, and shooting up the field from last to twenty-fifth place.

The Himalayas were still far away but the going was fearsome. The car was manhandled across rivers by eager locals, hoicked up banks on poles and pushed-and-pulled over boulder-strewn ground in the foothills leading up to Simla. Photographs suggest that Young and Jones were anticipating the film *Fitzcarraldo* in which a steamboat is manhandled by similar sweating crowds across the Andes. The traditionally soggy brakes meanwhile became 'very marginal indeed' in Young's understated words, and a few days later the car could only slow its descents by bumping into alternate verges on the way down. It was kept going by a devoted vanload of mechanics with limitless rubber seals, bearings, wheel nuts and, providentially, an entire new brake drum, brought out from England, just in case. These were supplemented by old Minor parts from local garages which still serviced India's ageing population of the car. (Extraordinary as the little ex-episcopal saloon's adventure might seem from Britain, Minors were a familiar sight for locals – and still are.) Other spares were cannibalised from Morris Oxfords (made in India at the time under the name of Hindustan Ambassadors and by far the most common car on the country's roads); most were just a fraction too big, but they were shaved and ground to fit.

Repairs en route included a radiator which went on

hissing after scrupulous plugging. It turned out that a snake had looped itself down from a tree above the stalled car. By Aurangabad – where, at the poshest hotel, Young introduced Jones as the Archbishop of Canterbury – the Minor had risen to a remarkable ninth place, having overtaken fifty-eight cars. Now, though, the rally was overtaken by political events. Violent opponents of Prime Minister Indira Ghandi targeted it to get publicity, causing diversions which made a muddle of the running order. Then a mob stoned the cars near Agra, and one man fired a starting pistol through the shattered windscreen of the leading Opel driven by the most popular rally driver in India at the time, the Kenyan Shekhar Mehta. A curtailed final leg saw the Minor gasp to over 10,000ft up the Himalayas before slithering down with its wrecked brake drums and the useless pedal flush with the floor. It crossed the finishing line in fifteenth place, but first in its small-car class.

Young and Jones were given silver medals by Mrs Ghandi and returned to Britain and a flurry of publicity, including a TV appearance that was nearly scuppered when the BBC tried to insist on covering the car's sponsorship transfers with fake mud. The Minor did a brief tour of shows, still with drifts of Indian dust inside the engine compartment and an untouched tin of boiled sweets taped to the parcel shelf. When Young tried to chip one of these out of the ball into which the heat of the rally had congealed them, a Morris Minor Owners Club member rushed over and warned him not to touch anything because the car was historic and famous and about to be preserved.

So it proved (though Young got his sweetie), but it was not Lord Montagu's museum which housed it in the end. They already had a Minor and decided that one was enough. The car was sent to Christie's before would-be British buyers had a chance to sort out bids and sold to a New Zealand museum for £1,300 (£3,800 today). There was a happy sequel. When Dr Runcie paid a visit to Christchurch some years later, he was welcomed at the airport with a red carpet and an official who told him: 'Come this way, your Grace, your car is waiting.' It was the battered old Minor which he had last driven round the fountain at Lambeth Palace before it sallied forth for its heroics. A home-made New Zealand numberplate had been tied with string to the bumpers so that he could take it for another spin, into Christchurch. He did, and it is still there in the museum.

The Archbishop's Minor was at the back of Tony Manos's mind when he came across an amateur version of the celebrated Paris–Dakar rally on the internet. Many years before, at the age of twenty-three, he had crossed the Sahara with his wife Geraldine in a four-wheel drive en route to a new job in South Africa. The idea of tackling something similar in a Morris Minor had been in his mind for a while. Modern 4×4s had taken a lot of the challenge out of rough driving overseas, he reckoned. He had also got as far as enlisting a co-driver in Chris Purren, a farmer from East Grinstead in Sussex who had diversified into holiday lets as agriculture became less profitable. The two men had been friends since kindergarten and got on well, crucial for anyone planning to share the interior of a Morris Minor for weeks in heat and dust. They were both laid-back and inclined to mind-wandering philosophy over a bottle of Jack Daniels. Tony had also read and much enjoyed *The Himalayan Minor*, and who should be leading the organisation of the Dakar expedition in 2005 but its author Philip Young, who had notched up many further rally successes and was now running the Endurance Rally Association.

'He was delighted at the idea that a Morris Minor should be involved,' says Manos, poking about in the engine compartment of MYD 633, where dust and grit from Mongolia still lies in small drifts. 'So I thought I had better set about trying to find one.' He had never been a petrolhead or a particular Morris Minor enthusiast – indeed had never owned or even driven one. Like me, his first solo outings had been in a Triumph Herald (coincidentally also in Leeds, where he studied mining engineering at the university). The Herald he drove had a particular advantage. His brother had rolled it on a youthful excursion to the West Country, and repairs had left the car with neither roof nor windscreen; 'as a result, it was just low enough to get under the car park barrier at the Henry Price student residences, where I lived,' saving him a lot of parking meter money.

He also enjoyed driving, and his engineering background gave him the skills to cope with basic repairs and maintenance on a car as straightforward as the Minor. He had practised on the Herald and on a stately Triumph Renown with huge headlamps and running boards which he bought for £15 from a friend at Mars chocolate factory in Slough, where he did holiday jobs. It finally perished in circumstances which also prepared Manos for his later-life rallying career. His mother ran a nursery school in Sutton, and the children found a way of unscrewing the Renown's non-lockable petrol cap and feeding gravel from the drive into the tank.

Manos set to work on MYD 633 after the drive from Wisbech, hunting around for a reconditioned Sprite engine to install, as had been done to the archbishop's car. He spent several months in a strange world where people selling reconditioned engines were only interested in buyers who had a worn-out old one for them to take on as their next project. It reminded me of negotiations I conducted as a student with a fitter at RAF Benson, who had a BSA Beagle motorbike for sale but would only accept an offer that included a 35mm film projector. I failed to find one, and so never got the bike, but Tony did eventually track down a garage in North London which sold him a pepped-up Sprite engine. He had a new gearbox put in, and disc brakes to replace the usual means of gliding to a leisurely halt. And then he sent off his entry form for the grandly named World Cup 2005.

Tony enjoyed the mechanical side of his cars, but when he had started contemplating a long-distance rally in 2004, he wasn't thinking in terms of hours under the bonnet beneath a flaming sun. He wasn't interested, either, in the huge, prestige events like the Himalaya or the real Paris–Dakar, where cars are pretuned for months and accompanied by teams of mechanics, these days often in helicopters. The Endurance Rally Association's version used Monte Carlo-style boot plates (which are still on the car, along with the flags of the countries they drove through), but the excursion was really for what Tony calls 'motoring enthusiasts who have no great back-up but want to have a go at rallying'.

A sweep car followed behind and checked every evening that all the cars were safely in, rather like the company rep on Saga rambling or skiing holidays.

It turned out to be a great mix of people – some took it seriously, others like us stopped and had sandwiches because the view was exceptionally good. It was really quite comfy with nice hotels – a gentleman's rally. There was one car whose owners had spent £30,000 in preparation and were not completely chuffed to find themselves lining up alongside an old Moggy, but most of the entrants rubbed along.

Tony unfolds a worn and torn map of the route on his kitchen table in Haslemere, which brings it all back. 'A mixture of old chaps living the dream and guys escaping the wife.'

'Except when they needed spares,' chips in Geraldine, who is making us a tasty lasagne on the Aga – and she did indeed play a crucial role. Like Lady Shackleton, who was asked by Sir Ernest from the Antarctic to start fund-raising for a new ship after one of his disasters, she took a call early in the adventure saying: 'We need front axle bearings.

Please meet us in Marrakech.' Morocco wasn't a bad place to take a mini-break, and Mrs Manos flew out, carrying an unexpectedly large amount of baggage. Word had got round the drivers that someone was coming from the UK with spares, and Tony was besieged with orders.

> She eventually tottered into the hotel with a heap of boxes, after charming her way through customs. One of the packages was a great big cylinder tube for another car, and they were naturally suspicious, with terrorism and the rest of it.

'What was it?' the officials wanted to know, and Geraldine had no idea.

> I just said 'It's something to do with a car' and made brrrm-brrrm and hooting noises. I think the customs guy just had enough of me, because he waved me impatiently through.

The next day, the son of another driver, who took out more parts and gave the customs a neat manifest, was charged £800 in duty.

Geraldine remembers looking round the Marrakech hotel and thinking back to packing tents and roughing-it gear for the trip. 'Nice place you've got here, boys,' she said, and Tony admits: 'In Africa we didn't use the tents once.' But the rally wasn't a doddle. Four cars overturned in the Atlas mountains, and the Minor was exempted from one trial section on the route, a ravine carved out by a vanished river, because the organisers were sure that it would never climb out. 'If I'd seen the conditions before we went, I probably wouldn't have gone by Morris Minor,' says Tony, but the car had one major advantage. African truckers played chicken with the rally cars, forcing them off the narrow metalled roads through Mauretania and Senegal, but the Minor worked its magic even on them.

> Initially they realised we weren't local and they weren't going to give way, but as they got closer they saw the car's unusual lines and, I guess, realised it wasn't a threat. Maybe they even went 'Aaaah!' – but, anyway, they were the ones who pulled off.

As a light car, the Minor also bounced across the sand that underlay much of the route more easily than the heavy 4×4s.

Tony and Chris were content with a stately pace and so came last-but-one out of fifty-seven, avoiding the wooden spoon only because a BMW belonging to a father-and-son team took such a hammering that it fell apart. A film of the rally focuses on drivers who accelerated away in the top ten cars, but each daily instalment shows the good old Minor come plugging in at the tail of the field, a slowcoach undoubtedly, but much less badly battered than the others. Even so, the attrition of unmade, boulder-strewn roads was a useful lesson for Tony's future plans. He spent much of the journey tightening bolts that kept being shaken undone. When MYD 633 rolled into Dakar, he had come to a simple conclusion. 'We had got there, but Africa isn't Morris country.'

Where is? Apart from Haslemere, where Tony pootled about on his return from Dakar and got to know the other local Minors: a black saloon, a pale green van in Liphook and a smart convertible in vanilla with a red top. Looking for new challenges, he lighted on a website called The Adventurist, which had organised a trans-India race in Tuk-Tuk taxis and a crossing of the English Channel in bouncy castles. It was advertising the third year of the Mongolia Run, a DIY rally you could only enter by hitting the website at a specified time and date. Needless to say, everything crashed as six thousand hopefuls clicked simultaneously, and on a rerun the rally was booked out in under three seconds. Tony wasn't lucky, but, with Dakar under his belt, decided to go it alone anyway. The Minor had been refettled and now boasted its pattern of daisy transfers, after the marriage of Tony and Geraldine's daughter, who used DYM 633 as her wedding car.

This was a good omen, thought Tony, adding to the Minor's innocuous appeal which had softened the lorry drivers in Africa. Corrupt police and sticky government officials in the former Soviet Union would also be disarmed, he hoped, by the fact that the travellers were 'two old farts' (given the Minor's exhaust noises, that should really be three). After a party in Prague and the promise of another in Ulan Bator, where the official rally was due to arrive two weeks later, the intrepid little trio set off.

Poland and the Czech Republic were fine, Ukraine was a hole and Russia very aggressive, but things didn't get really wild until Kazakhstan. It was like Borat on speed, completely wacky and full of things you don't ever see in Haslemere.

'Like Essex?' hazards Geraldine, who this time had been way beyond the range of plaintive appeals for spare parts. 'Well it wasn't the place for women who want hair-straighteners,' counters Tony.

Life was Spartan. Driving an average of twelve hours a day (no joke in a Morris Minor) the two men took a tent each, sleeping bags and two changes of clothes – which, even with the back seat stripped out, left little room for anything else apart from emergency food and spares. Both have bad backs, but their Recaro rally seats, copied from Philip Young's Church of England car, eased the pain. They became masters of their zip-open, pop-up tents, and by the Kazak border reckoned to reach the Jack Daniels every evening within half-an-hour.

Flying ahead of the real rally, they had no fixed route and relied on local knowledge, a compass and the fact that Ulan Bator was always east. 'We were a little Morris Minor creeping across the face of the world,' says Tony. 'All we knew was where we were headed.' Luckily, the Kazakhs were only too eager to give a hand. 'The one thing you won't see in Kazakhstan is a Morris Minor, and everyone wants to help you, even the police.' Notorious for wanting bribes, traffic officers leapt into the car's path with lollipop batons, but then insisted only on a twenty-minute tour beneath the bonnet.

They were all mechanically-minded because they have to keep their own cars on the road, mostly big old Ladas. They'd open the bonnet and laugh and say 'Where's the engine? Where is everything? Why is it *so* small?' They had a lot of admiration for British engineering from the Morris Minor period. Their line was: 'British cars in those days – you knew how to do it. Simplicity, quality and appealing. A perfect piece of design. That's what you had.' I can't think of another car that would engender the same response from your average Kazakh policeman.

It was lucky the police were so entranced, because the Minor had a large number of quirks, including the fact that connecting the new Sprite engine had dished the dashboard control panels. Tony and Chris didn't know the petrol level or their speed, and a 1951 Minor like DYM 633 didn't have a temperature gauge. 'The original dashboard was pretty sparse, but none of ours worked,' says Tony. 'We just got to know by experience how fast we were going and how much fuel was left.' It was ten thousand miles to Ulan Bator, double the run to Dakar and on equally awful tracks in Mongolia and parts of Kazakhstan. As Tony says, 'You couldn't put a Minor through that and expect things not to happen.' They had three days of handbrake driving after the main brake pipe sheared, until they arrived at a tiny town distinguished by having a fire station. They stopped and asked if there was a mechanic, and the firemen were ecstatic. They jacked the car up in no time, examined the entire engine and transmission, took the wheels off, greased and oiled all the moving bits and refused to take more than £25.

On they crept. A thousand-mile detour had to be made back to Almaty when their visas were refused at the border into far Eastern Russia (again, the Minor melted the heart of an initially stony Russian consul in the Kazakh capital). Feeling like a lonely space probe themselves, they passed the isolated, debris-surrounded Soviet space centre at Baikonur. Across the Mongolian border they found a dry riverbed swollen to a forty-foot-wide torrent, impassable until two teenage shepherds guided them by hand signals to a rickety, submerged ford. They inched across, the exhaust bubbling underwater for part of the time, and a steep drop down to the riverbed only a couple of stones' width away. When the official rally arrived a fortnight later, several cars floated away downstream. Sedan-chair poles came to the rescue across marshes which followed, and then the car hit the mountains of western Mongolia with a thump. A gravelly incline was so steep that Tony fitted new spark plugs, cleaned all the points, revved to maximum and took a run at it. He stopped just in time at the top to avoid taking off and crash-landing on the sump. Ahead of the car stretched empty plains leading on to the Gobi desert. For one day after leaving the town of Khovd, the provincial capital at the foot of the Altai mountains, he and Chris saw no one at all. 'It was a wonderful place to be philosophical,' says Tony.

'That's why you do it. Just the two of you driving a Morris Minor across a vast desert is a remarkable experience. We're so used to being in control, and here we emphatically weren't.' Police checks continued regularly, on Kazakh lines, but all the bored officers ever wanted to do was find out what the car was and be photographed standing beside it.

At other times, herdsmen would materialise in the empty landscape, or a boulder-strewn track would turn out to be a diversion from the main, unmarked, way and peter out in a circle of yurts. The car must have appeared to the nomad communities to be some sort of motorised yurt itself. Its rounded shape reflected the structure of their tent homes. But, as the last leg of the marathon approached, DYM 633 was cracking up. Bolts sheared repeatedly from the rear shock absorbers until the latter were useless and juddering against the frame of the car. In a lonely village a mechanic welded them on to the chassis, but gradually the strain of the repeated bumps and jolts spread to the body. The car started splitting open above the petrol tank. Tony and Chris changed tactic and removed the shock absorbers altogether as the car bounced onwards to Ulan Bator. It was direly uncomfortable, but the Minor stayed in one piece. 'It was right for the purpose for which it was actually built,' says Tony, adding in wonderment: 'But abuse it to the extent that we abused it, and it just keeps on going.'

Still two weeks ahead of the official Adventurists, they arrived in the Mongolian capital without ceremony and spent their first evening discreetly mopping up a pond of oil in the hotel car park. The sump had finally expired as they drove into town, and oil was spewing out everywhere by the time they pulled up. With the holes partly sealed by an 'instant metal' paste, they left the car at last and headed for the main square. Here they ended up celebrating at the weekly quiz night in the local 'English Pub' – a strangely Haslemere-like end to their extraordinary journey. The next morning DYM 633, with her cheerful daisies just showing through the dust, was driven into a container after charming one last bureaucrat. An unsmiling woman customs officer had discovered that details in the logbook and on the chassis did not match, because of an error. She was minded to stop the shipment to China, from where the car was due to go on to Tilbury docks and home; but then she saw the Minor, and her heart softened.

All that was left was to play a little engineers' game. The sump was sealed but oil was dripping through one small unblocked hole. Checking the rate of drips and the length of the voyage, Tony Manos worked out the size of the pool of oil in the container which would greet him when he and DYM 633 were reunited. Then he flew back and started thinking about the next big adventure, maybe in a couple of years' time. 'Morris Minors seem to be able to go on for ever,' he says. That was a chance remark of Tony's but one full of foresight, and it raises the last big question about the Morris Minor.

Chapter 10
The Durable Car Company

Why can't cars last as long as houses?

Charles Ware, *Today*, 1986

CHARLES WARE'S VISION OF cars lasting for years, conceivably indefinitely, has a symbol in his office: a green apple which looks as though it has been overlooked at lunchtime and then got slightly bruised. Balancing on one of the few spaces not occupied by paper or Minor memorabilia, including a bottle of Old Moggy ale, it turns out on closer inspection to be the 2003 Green Apple Award for environmental contributions to the motor industry, which Ware and his Morris Minor Centre were given at the House of Commons by the then Secretary of State for Trade and Industry, Patricia Hewitt. The citation acknowledged the little firm's work on creating a type of car whose 'green' credentials arguably put much more modern innovations, such as the hybrid Toyota Prius, in the shade. This is the Series 3 Morris Minor, cheekily named by Charlie to give the impression that it continues the car's official line of production, which actually stopped at Cowley in 1971.

There are not very many Series 3s on the road, for all that

the prototype appeared as long ago as 1985. At the time it was much discussed in the motoring press as 'A Minor re-engineered for the Eighties' – and in Germany under equivalent headlines like 'Ein Morris Minor Serie 3 fur dir achtziger Jahre' or France where *La Vie de l'Auto* ran a piece headed: 'Morris Minor: Voiture du Futur?' The trial vehicle was a 1960s Traveller which came into Charlie's workshops in the early 1980s as a sadly run-down rustbucket with rotting timber and no MOT certificate; it was worth less than £100. Bit by bit, the worn-out parts and panels were replaced, while a transformation took place in the engine, transmission and gears. Much of the work was contracted to a specialist firm in Bristol, A.D. Engineering, who fitted a 1275cc BMC A-Series engine, a Spridget gearbox and a Morris Ital rear axle. The car was given Marina disc brakes instead of the spongy old originals that have rendered many Minor drivers white-faced as their right foot seemed to disappear into the floor. The aim, Ware explained in his accompanying booklet *Durable Car Ownership*, was a care-fully-engineered, modernised version of the Minor, aimed at families, undaunted by motorways and challenging similar-sized new cars such as the Ford Fiesta on price.

At first hearing, this might sound a bit dippy, like the Monster Raving Loony Alliance Party's manifesto in Cambridge at the last election, which promised to bring back the Morris Minor as part of a slate of transport reforms. Candidate Nicholas Brettell-Winnington neatly combined nostalgia and modern improvements, very much in the Ware style, when he pledged:

The Morris Minor with an 1100 engine, but with original chrome and split windscreen, will be reintroduced on a mass-production basis. State funding of the provision of mass-produced easily accessible vehicles which can be adapted for disabled use will give real mobility to the people, and undermine the expensive import car market.

He concluded the section with a reference to Communist East Germany's cheap and simple (albeit highly polluting) car: 'Look, if the Trabant can achieve cult status . . .'

Actually, the Raving Loonies often make very sensible suggestions. They were very quick to cotton on to legitimising pirate radio stations and lowering the voting age, and my two sons backed their candidate in a by-election for Bradford North because of his logical approach to the name of a famous roundabout in the suburb of Idle (home of the even more famous Idle Working Men's Club) called Five Lane Ends. A new Morrison's supermarket had just been built, with its own slip road on to the roundabout. The Loony candidate said that if he won, he would rename the place Six Lane Ends. He didn't, and it wasn't – but my sons have always felt that he was right.

The theory of durable car ownership is also logical: a simple transfer to cars of the principle that guided Ware's successful work as a property developer. If you have got something old and well built, why destroy it? Like a Georgian house, he argues, a Morris Minor represents excellent value in terms of the materials used to make it. It dates from an era when goods were cheaper and wages lower and before built-in obsolescence became an acceptable way of manufacturing. Like an old house, it needs regular and careful maintenance, but when this is offset against the removal of depreciation from the sums – because Minors are now almost certain to increase in value with age – the result is Mr Micawber's happiness. Old models also need modern adaptations unless you like driving in an echoing metal can with poor emissions and few safety backups. But these are easily remedied. Ware uses another analogy with restoring houses, arguing that adding electronic ignition, two-speed wipers or a reversing light is the equivalent of fitting central heating.

The Series 3 prototype embodied these principles, and in 1985 Ware wheeled it out for the motoring press, cheered by the sight of BBC radio's Hugh Sykes, who travelled around in his own two-door Morris Minor. The journalists were intrigued and, by and large, convinced that the project could find a commercial market, albeit a modest one. *Autocar* had initial problems with their electronic testing gear: there was no cigar lighter to plug it into. But their review began by describing the car, WAH 793H, as 'a seemingly unpretentious Morris Minor Traveller, the kind your Auntie always ran around in', and ended by christening it 'The Mighty Wah'. The writer Matthew Carter contrasted the trials and discomforts of driving a conventional Minor with WAH's purring ride in comfy seats – commissioned from the specialist firm Callow and Maddox – and the astonishment it left on the faces of drivers in a Ford Capri, an MG Midget and a BMW 528i who were respectively beaten off the lights in Wells and overtaken on the M3. Paul Skilleter of *Practical Classics* magazine concluded that WAH was in a totally different class from the standard Minor and added, crucially for Ware's hopes: 'Personally, I'd rate it ahead of a typical modern hatchback or Astra.'

There was one bad fairy at the feast, the environmental journalist Richard North, who complained with some reason in *The Times* that the Morris Minor was becoming what he called an 'Uncar'. Cutting up rough, he mocked what he described as 'the horrible little virtues of the Morris Minor' and accused many of its new buyers of being hypocrites who didn't want to be thought of as owning cars.

> Hip young people flock to buy cosy old Minors so as to have somewhere appropriate to sport their 'Nuclear power? No thanks!' stickers. The only good car is a taxi, as anyone in smug possession of a few bikes and a British Rail Familycard will tell you.

The *Sunday Telegraph* raised an eyebrow over the notion of spending the £10,000 for which WAH was insured on a car whose basic design was nearly half a century old. But its reporter David Shannon continued wistfully: 'The charm, beauty and durability of the Minor and the availability and cheapness of spare parts for it make it easy to be persuaded otherwise.' Soon after interviewing Ware, he bought a car – a Morris Minor.

It was not a Series 3, though. Apart from WAH, there

were none of those actually available off-the-peg, and in the years since 1985 Ware's hopes of realising his ideal by starting an actual production line have been frustrated. The nearest he got, he says, was later in the 1980s, when a subsidiary of Japanese Airlines got in touch to discuss the notion of large-scale production of the Series 3, or something like it, in Japan. Famously fond of Beatrix Potter and the Brontës, the Japanese were seen by the company as ripe for an Olde English car, especially the Traveller (at which Dame Edna Everage had exclaimed so delightedly on her TV profile of Stratford upon Avon: 'Look possums! Even the cars are half-timbered!') The new Minors would have been built in Coventry at the old Reliant works, says Ware, and the Japanese talked about producing three thousand a year and investing £25 million. 'It would have been wonderful, very exciting,' he says, as we finally finish our mugs of tea and head back to the Brislington centre in the borrowed Traveller. 'The name wasn't for sale, and so it never came to anything. But it's still a huge idea. Producing Morris Minors with the latest technology, that would be the way to go.'

Instead, the Series 3 philosophy has been incorporated into the Morris Minor Centre's core business of renovating and updating customers' cars. The current brochure offers three pages of 'Series 3 updates', which range from much more powerful Halogen headlights to radio and CD player and even – *Autocar* would be pleased to discover – a cigar lighter which doubles as a mobile phone charger. New mixes with old in extras such as an electric front and rear windscreen washer kit, which comes with a 'period-style switch' on the dash. More fundamentally, you can have a five-speed gearbox based on the Ford Sierra's fitted, or reconditioned 1275cc engines, which hike the standard unit up by nearly 200cc and run on unleaded petrol. All have the bonus of being exempt from road tax because of their age. Parts, if not always cheap, remain as available as they were when David Shannon was seduced in 1986, and the other great guarantee for people wanting their Minor to last for ever is a supply of newly-made body panels. This played a part in Ware's award of that wooden Green Apple in his office, and to understand it, you have to travel 5,500 miles to the other side of the world.

Welcome to Galle in southern Sri Lanka, home of cricket Tests, where a large shed consisting of a tin roof supported by palm-tree trunks is the home of The Durable Car Company. Founded by a retired Sri Lankan diplomat, Dhanapala Samarasekara, this is the exotic, if small-scale, equivalent for Ware of what Pressed Steel at Oxford was for Lord Nuffield in his heyday. From inside the building comes a battery of clangs and thunks, the unmistakeable sound of hammer and gavel on Morris Minor body parts. Wings, doors and bonnets destined for Bath are manufactured at a gentle but steady rate by thirty-five staff who have also developed tools and jigs for at least eighty Minor components. Local wages went up by fifty per cent when the factory opened in 1991, says Ware, and each worker plays a central part in supporting an average extended family of fifteen people. Samarasekara has modest expansion plans for a small tourist resort in the neighbouring village, with solar power, sustainable building materials, organic gardening and the prospect of extra income for Durable Car Company workers' families. The land has been in his family for generations, and the house where he grew up still stands across a rice paddy from the factory. He has happy memories of playing there as a boy and developing a passion for keeping bees, which played a part in teaching him the value of organisation and hard work. But he is also canny. As a young man, he was involved with left-wing activists, and a side benefit came in the form of tip-offs about strikes that were likely to affect the Samarasekara tea-growing estate. The regime at Galle is a mixture of idealism, nous and a fierce pride in local handicraft and metal-working skills. Every product is stamped 'Hand-made in Sri Lanka'.

It is also significant that the workers in Galle are not involved in the mass-production of some curious Western object, like Chinese factory staff making Easter chicks or Tellytubby models. Sri Lanka and its subcontinent neighbours India and Pakistan anticipated Charles Ware by some years in the concept of durable car ownership, notably with the Morris Minor. Ancient models have been kept in daily use for decades, a situation little changed since Philip Young and the crew behind the Archbishop of Canterbury's Minor discovered plentiful local expertise during the 1980 Himalayan Rally. Thousands of Minors are still in daily use in Sri Lanka, not as classic cars but as essential workhorses, taxis and runabouts with the family crammed in the back.

The island also has enthusiastic members of the Morris Minor Club and regular Morris Minor races; traditionally, tournaments of older cars begin with a Minor class hurtling round the international motor-racing track at Pannala at 70mph-plus.

As with Ware's first Morris Minor initiative in Bath back in 1976, competition has started up too. During the 1980s a Danish enthusiast, Anton Kamp Nielsen, developed a small sideline in supplying Morris Minor parts, initially from a 1961 two-door saloon and then from old wrecks which in some cases he took, free, off despairing owners' hands. In 1992 he visited Sri Lanka and saw the hosts of old Minors in action; three years later, he set up Classic Cars (Pvt) on the island and by 2005 was producing some five hundred different components, announcing charmingly on the firm's website. 'It is a pleasure to make it possible for the Morris Minor Owner to have a good time doing his car.' He also praised Sri Lanka's pleasant climate compared with northern Europe, and was quick to see the potential in links between a collection of Morris Minors and the island's tourism industry. His plant forged particular links with the Happy Banana hotel at Unawatuna near Galle, which promised 'extra good service' to guests who mentioned Morris Minors. A local Morris Minor taxi was also available, protecting inexperienced tourists from touts, although the longer journey to the airport had to be done by Toyota.

A new van with a fibreglass body was produced in 2003, cannibalising old Minors and aiming at a possible gap in the local market. Morris Minor vans are not common in Sri

Lanka, and the pick-up version was never exported there. There were plenty of modern rivals, but Nielsen reckoned that the Minor's robustness could have the edge in tasks such as ferrying oil drums or gas cylinders along bumpy local roads. Also, new seat trims are turned out on sewing machines, new woodwork made for Travellers, and a children's pedal-car Minor has been produced. When the tsunami struck the island on Boxing Day in 2005 the company's premises were just far enough inland to escape – the wave stopped less than two miles away – and it was able to provide generous, targeted help. Many people known to Anton and his staff died in the tragedy, and the Happy Banana was devastated, but is now back in action.

This year the company organised a Morris Minor rally starting from Galle fort at the end of January, travelling through the town in a stately convoy and ending up with a feast at the company's headquarters. A sequence of clips on YouTube shows the poached eggs enjoying a sweltering day, most of them black but including a dashing white saloon with blue slashes across the front passenger doors, one of the fibreglass-bodied vans and a bright mauve convertible which brought up the rear. There was also a yellow Mini-Moke, which failed to stay the course. All the Minors did, apart from two which broke down on the way to the rendezvous at Galle. Anton is considering a second rally on 25 January 2009 and in future years, and invites anyone to join in, free. 'It takes three to four weeks of driving (from western Europe) if you dare,' he says, 'and there is a ninety-nine per cent chance of 30°C plus and sunshine.'

*

These delightful goings-on in Sri Lanka, and the successful work of Charles Ware and other Minor rebuilders in Britain, mean that the car has a guaranteed future on the world's roads for many years in – appropriately – a minor way. But it would be unrealistic not to recognise that these cars depend for their existence on the larger market that Ware takes to task in his Durable Car philosophy. Like the apparently retro Morgan sports car, with its hidden engine taken from Land Rover or BMW, they rely on other marques for their power units, and often gearboxes and other components too. The larger question for Minor enthusiasts is whether a completely new Morris Minor might take to the roads one day, echoing the grand old car in styling perhaps, but otherwise taking it into the twenty-first century. We have seen the new Beetle and the new Mini, and in its day, the 1948 Minor revived a name originally given to William Morris's first counter-attack on the Austin Seven: the original Minor produced at Cowley between 1928 and 1934.

Some cynics have suggested that the new Minor has already appeared in the shape of the Volkswagen Polo, a sturdy, cheap and reliable runabout, albeit a little short of cosy charm. But could the big motor manufacturers be tempted to revive the Morris Minor name? Was there an omen, wonders Charlie Ware, when he tried to buy it or get it on licence from BMW for his planned mass production in harness with Japanese Airlines, and failed?

The potential decision has long since passed out of the

hands of BMW, which sold the rights to the Morris Minor name as part of its disposal of the Rover Group to the Phoenix Consortium of four Midlands businessmen in 2000 for a nominal £10. The deal ended six unhappy years during which the German company had tried but failed to revive the grand old name of Rover. Because of legal complications involving redundancy law, and in a jingoistic atmosphere at the prospect of a major car-making company returning to British hands again, BMW actually guaranteed an interest-free loan of £427 million to keep the firm's Longbridge plant going and save 8000 jobs. It was the economics of Wonderland, apart from BMW's sensible retention of the Mini, and in 2005 Phoenix went into liquidation. More agonising followed, until later the same year, the remaining assets were bought for £53 million by the state-owned Nanjing Automobile Corporation of China.

Thus it is that the future of the ultimate English car is now in the hands of the Beijing government, albeit any decision would be made by technocrats and marketing specialists in Nanjing and Longbridge. Asking around, I heard surprisingly warm comments about the new owners of the Birmingham plant. They might be foreign – indeed extremely foreign, in terms of sheer physical distance – but they were approachable, friendly and aware of the history behind their apparently bedraggled British acquisition. So I was told, and so it proved when I got in touch with the company at Longbridge, which Nanjing has made the headquarters of its new subsidiary NAC MG UK. Within hours the firm's Customer Relationships Manager, Keith

Harris, was back to me, setting out Nanjing's approach to the possibility of a Minor return.

The company has yet to celebrate its third anniversary but it has not gone short of advice about reviving the marque. The original Minor is, after all, in many ways a car version of the simple, sturdy, endlessly reliable Flying Pigeon bicycles everyone in China seemed to ride in the days of Chairman Mao. Enthusiasts' websites regularly debate the issue, and the main MG Rover fans forum includes a special thread entitled Messages to Nanjing, for Harris and his colleagues to read. Bloggers line up on both sides. One, with the online name Streetrover, calls the Minor 'as much a fun car as the Mini' and therefore equally worth reviving. Peterover agrees:

> I love the idea of a new Morris Minor, but not a cuddly retro mobile. Instead, a forward-thinking car that redefines the family car sector as the original did in its day. It is internationally popular, and the use of the name will in itself create widespread interest, à la BMW Mini.

Not so, reckons SopwithUK, who counters:

> I completely disagree with reviving old brands like Austin and making a new Morris Minor. First thing that comes to mind with Austin are rubbish cars like the Maestro, Montego and Allegro, and the Minor was so long ago that I don't think anyone would want a modern one.

Well . . . BMW's New Mini is selling well – increasingly so, now that fuel prices and green taxes are hitting bigger and more gas-guzzling makes of car. And I hope that this book has proved by now that the Morris Minor name and reputation is far from the stuff of 'so long ago'. Harris seemed to be sympathetic too. He told me, among other things, that he worked with a goodly number of classic car buffs and enthusiasts, and Nanjing is clearly well aware of the potential value of the dormant marques it acquired with the MG Rover takeover. These include every car name branded in the past by Austin, Morris, Wolseley and Standard, as well as MG, which is currently the focus of the firm's British activities.

There have not – yet – been any detailed discussions from a marketing point of view about the possible use of any of them, apart from MG. Keith Harris elaborated:

It is simply impossible at this stage to legitimately rule the use of any other brand either in or out for Longbridge-produced cars over the long term. (By the long term I mean in excess of five years. Our business plan until then is certainly only focused on the development of the MG marque.)

One thing at a time, then, but remember how long it took for Issigonis's lightweight sports car drawings of the mid-1930s to make it into production in 1948 as the first Morris Minor Series MM. Harris kindly speculated that his classic-car-buff colleagues would want to add this book to their shelves, and if so, I would like to end it with a message to them, and to their superiors in Nanjing and Beijing.

When I visited China myself some years ago, I was very impressed by the Flying Pigeons. Their simple sturdiness reminded me exactly of the Morris Minor. Since then, Chinese bikes have developed all the gears and gizmos of the Western counterparts – just as Nanjing now makes more than four hundred types of car, van and lorry, instead of the limited, straight-up-and-down range of Maoist times. But the underlying principles, the Morris Minor principles, remain, as they do for so many of us in the UK. The car has proved itself again and again out East, creating the sort of traditions necessary to underpin a 'New Minor' launch in the markets of China, Indonesia or the Malay peninsular. And there is a wider attraction.

There are many ways of smoothing the path of international relations, and sometimes they can shine imaginatively through the routine procedures of diplomacy. Beijing and London are bound to have increasingly close dealings, politically and even more in trade and finance, where China's vast superiority in size is matched by Britain's expertise. As a sweetener for any of that sourness that inevitably affects relationships from time to time, could there be anything finer than a China Minor? I bet that millions of us in Britain would buy one.

Epilogue

 In the days when I drove a Morris Minor, I used to potter about, seldom taking the quickest route from A to B and never cruising at 70 mph along a motorway as we do these days. Here at journey's end, I am conscious that this book has adopted something of the same style. I hope the meanderings between past and present, the here-and-now and history, have not tried your patience, and that you have been able to relax into the same unhurried mood.

We did start at a sort of A, and perhaps came round to it again at the end, for the Morris Minor shows every sign of going on and on. It is a rare car – indeed a rare creation – which attracts almost universal affection, but this is such a one. I have been fascinated to learn how many years went into its creation in the mind of Issigonis, and how much was required of Sir Miles Thomas in the way of negotiating skills. I have been astonished to find how far Minors have travelled across the world, and delighted to share the company of those who own or remember them. I specially enjoyed hearing about Bridget Johnson's Traveller fungus.

And now I have one last job: getting out there and buying one again for Penny and myself, all these years after UMU 431 F went to a new home. There are four runners on eBay as I write, ranging from a snappy-looking convertible for £4,700 to a 1968 saloon which was driven into a shed in Taunton two years ago and, according to the owner, 'may need a bit of fuel to start again now . . .' Or I can beat a top bid of 99p for a Traveller front bumper (including cover) and use that as the basis of a slow and leisurely rebuild. It's my birthday soon, and Penny's not long afterward. Thank you for helping, by buying or borrowing this book.

Postscript

Marie Lorimer, who provided this book's index, attached her work to an email which summarises in a few lines much of what I have tried to say about the Minor as Britain's favourite car. She wrote:

> I won't let my husband get his hands on this book as I know what will happen. He had a Minor when we were students – every panel painted a different colour and a garden gnome welded on top (well, it was the 1970s). We used to go from the South up to Manchester every term-time and in the cold weather had to drum our feet on the floor to keep warm (no heater, and one front window jammed permanently down). I had two – my second, pale blue, was stolen and ended up in a park lake.

I rest my case.

Select bibliography

Books

Bardsley, Gillian, *Issigonis: The Official Biography*, Icon Books, 2005

Buchanan, C.D., *Mixed Blessing*, Leonard Hill Books, 1958

Caunter, C.F., *The History and Development of Light Cars*, HMSO, 1957

Chambers, Maurice; Turner, Stuart; Browning, Peter, *BMC Competitions Department Secrets*, Veloce Publishing, 2005

Dunnett, Peter J.S., *The Decline of the British Motor Industry*, Croom Helm, 1980

Moss, Pat, *The Story So Far*, William Kimber, 1967

Pender, Karen, *The Secret Life of the Morris Minor*, Veloce, 1995

Thomas, Sir Miles, *Out on a Wing*, Michael Joseph, 1964

Turner, Graham, *The Car Makers*, Eyre & Spottiswoode, 1963

—— *The Leyland Papers*, Eyre & Spottiswoode, 1971

Ware, Charles, *The Morris Minor Centre 1976–87, The First Ten Years*, Morris Minor Centre, 1987

Young, Philip, *The Himalayan Minor*, Speedwell Books, 1987

Websites

MMOC: *www.morrisminoroc.co.uk* The foremost club site in the world. Plentiful public information but a gold mine if you join the club.

Minor Mania: *www.minormania.com* The inspired website of a New Zealand enthusiast with an eye for the extraordinary as well as routine.

Charlie Ware Morris Minor centre: *www.morrisminor.org.uk* The biggest of such specialists (of whom there are many).

Sri Lankan Minors: *www.morrisminor.org.uk* Masses of info about Anton Kamp Nielsen's operation in the sun.

Military Minors: *www.militaryminors.tk* Site under construction as we went to press, but has some info and is linked to a site for Minor vans ('Freezing in winter, unbearable in summer . . .').

Morris Minor Clinic: *www.morrisminorclinic.co.uk* Home of Mick Pelling and his beast.

Index